F

A

Phenomenal

I

T

H

BFF PUBLISHING HOUSE

BFF Publishing House is a Limited Liability Corporation dedicated wholly to the appreciation and publication of books for children and adults for the advancement of diversification in literature.

For more information on publishing contact:

Antionette Mutcherson at

bff@bffpublishinghouse.com

Website: bffpublishinghouse.com

Published in the United States by

BFF Publishing House

Atlanta, Georgia First Edition, 2022

Contents

Chapter 1

Immense Pain Leads to Inspiring Purpose

In 2019, I was living a very happy and fulfilled life. I was thirty-five years old, married with five beautiful children, and living in my dream home with an enjoyable career. My days were predictable, but busy. A typical week included attending events at the children's schools and their extracurricular activities, completing business analyses for work, and squeezing in time to write, blog, and be creative via my various passions. I enjoyed every moment of it. As a naturally driven and self-motivated person, I worked hard to create the life I wanted and took pride in accomplishing all the things I put my mind towards achieving.

I would take a few days every few months to travel with family or friends to a new destination to recharge my batteries. Those trips gave me something to look forward to and were a much-needed reprieve from my repetitive daily routines. My next trip was planned for March that year—a girl's trip to the beautiful beaches of Destin, Florida. A few days before I was to board the plane for my highly anticipated mini vacation, tragedy struck, and it would be the worst experience of my life. That day would literally change my life forever.

The Life-Changing Accident

March 17, 2019 was a pretty typical Sunday. My husband was out of town, and I spent the day with my children as I do most weekends. My goal for that day was to do laundry, buy groceries for the kids, and pack my bags so I could be stress-free in the days leading up to the five-day trip away from my family. As the of a large family, my life was always filled with meticulous planning to ensure everything went smoothly in the house. This weekend was no exception.

That morning, my cousin called me. His tone of voice expressed a combination of fear and urgency, and my ears immediately perked up to listen because I had never heard him sound like that before. He said, "Ebonee, I had the most horrible dream. I dreamed that you were in an ambulance and you were dying. The dream seemed so real that I had to call you and see if you were okay." I was startled by the dream, but assured him I was perfectly fine. He continued to share details about the dream, and I was amazed at the level of detail he remembered. After we ended the call, I thought about the things he said for a while, but eventually just put them in the back of my mind.

I was cleaning and packing well into the evening, and I lost track of time until my kids informed me they were hungry. I decided to make chicken strips and french fries, just something quick and easy to prepare so I could quickly get back to completing my weekend to-do list, as Monday was fast approaching. I put a pot of oil on the stove and turned on the burner. What happened from there became a blur of panic, adrenaline, and chaos. However, I will share what I can remember.

I remember the pot of cooking oil catching on fire. Huge flames burst from the oil in the pot. I still do not know what caused the fire. Possibly, some oil spilled down the side of the pot and caught fire on the stove. Maybe, some of the small ice particles from the cold fries hitting the hot oil caused the pot to catch fire. I do not know. The flames hit me in my face, burning underneath my chin, my lips, my cheeks, and other parts of my face. I believe the pain and shock of my burning face caused me to accidentally hit the handle of the pot of oil, knocking it off the stove, and hot oil spilled on my body. At that point, oil covered the tile floor, which caused me to slip, and my body landed in the hot oil! It all happened extremely fast, within seconds.

I started screaming as loudly as possible, "Someone call 911, please! I need help!" The fire alarm blared, repeating beeps and an automated female voice saying, "Fire, fire, fire!" Only three of my five children were in the house at that time. My younger kids, ages two and seven, were playing in the living room when the fire started. I am so grateful they were smart enough to run out the front door to the nearest neighbor's house. My oldest daughter, age seventeen, was upstairs, heard my screams, and called 911.

I ran into the bathroom. I had to see my face. It felt like my whole face had melted off, and I needed to see with my own eyes what it looked like rather than what I assumed in my head. I was so afraid of what I would see when I looked in the mirror, but I needed to know how bad it was. When I looked in the mirror, my skin looked a bit shiny and a bit darker, but the skin was not peeling off or blistering as burns tend to do. Even amid the pain, I felt relieved. I was confident my face would heal with minimal damage. However, what I saw in the mirror then was much different than what my face would look like weeks down the road.

I looked down at my exposed arms. Unlike my face, they were noticeably burnt. I kept thinking about my beach trip and how it was ruined because now I would be healing from burn wounds. With my adrenaline rushing and my mind racing, I had no understanding of the actual extent of damage this accident caused and the impact it would continue to have years into the future. I naively thought it would be something I would quickly heal from, which is why my thoughts went to my trip that I would miss rather than the fact that I would have a long and difficult recovery process ahead of me.

The ambulance came quickly. About four or five paramedics and firefighters came through my front door.

"Where is the fire, ma'am?"

I pointed to the kitchen, although there was no active fire anymore. I sat in my dining room chair, cried tears that burned my face even more, and felt so defeated. The paramedics began to cut my clothing off my body.

"Ma'am, I am not trying to expose you. I just need to see the extent of what is burned on your body."

I was not wearing a bra, so as he cut my shirt up the front from my waist to my neck, I saw my burned breasts and stomach. I started fading in and out of consciousness at this point. I could hear the paramedics talking to me, but it took so much effort for me to respond back to them—so much so that they had to repeat questions several times. I was confused as to what was happening. They loaded me into the ambulance, and I faded into a state that did not seem like reality. Everything started happening in slow motion, literally. At every turn of the ambulance, my body felt like it was floating fluidly in the direction of the turn. I seriously thought I was dying. I said to myself, "This is what it feels like to die."

I continued to hear the voices of the paramedics, but the voices sounded more like thoughts they were thinking inside their heads rather than conversations out loud. At every turn the ambulance made and every bump in the road we passed, I felt my body moving in slow motion. It was such a fluid movement, similar to the way gelatin wiggles, except in a much slower motion. My body felt so good at this point. I am sure they had given me medication to numb the pain. I felt my stress releasing into the atmosphere. All the pressure associated with my mental to-do list floated into the air—the assignments due at work, packing for my trip, preparing my children for the school week, bills, and all my responsibilities floated into the air. It was the most amazing feeling, and I wanted to stay in this state of no stress forever.

Upon arrival at the hospital, I was placed in a medically induced coma. I have very little memory of what transpired during my first few weeks there. I stayed in the Intensive Care Unit at San Antonio Military Medical Center (SAMMC) for the next three weeks. I had several surgeries, the first of which would be a debridement procedure to remove all the burned skin from my body. The surgeries that followed consisted of skin grafting—a process of removing healthy, non-burned skin from parts of my body and using it to cover the areas with third-degree burns. The places where the skin is removed are called donor sites. I had donor sites on my back, the left side of my stomach, the back of both of my thighs, and my right calf.

While in the ICU, I was placed on a machine that would breathe for me, called a ventilator. Doctors were worried that my body was not performing well with oral intubation and decided I needed a surgical hole in my neck, called a tracheostomy, so that a breathing tube could bypass my swollen upper airway. The tracheostomy would cause much frustration and even panic attacks when I became conscious, as it limited my ability to communicate and made me feel as if I was suffocating when I attempted physical activity.

I had so much support from family and friends while in the ICU. I had a vast support system made up of friends, church members, and coworkers. My husband visited me daily, and my dad drove from Alabama to Texas to be there for me in the hospital. Because I was in an induced coma, I do not remember many of the people who visited me and prayed over me. It would be months later, while having conversations with people, that they would inform me that they had visited me in the hospital, but I had absolutely no recollection of them being there. I am thankful for each person.

This situation showed me how loved I was by so many people, which I had never realized. It amazed me that people could rally together so efficiently to support my family by creating meal trains and taking turns bringing home-cooked meals and groceries to my kids. From the day of the accident, it was over a month until I would see my kids again. This was the longest time I had ever been apart from them, but my community helped to fill in the gap until I returned home.

Back to Life, Back to Reality

When I came to full consciousness, there was this thick haze covering my vision, almost like fog on a windshield in need of defrosting, but I could still make out that the person in front of me was my husband. He asked, "Do you know who I am?" I nodded yes. He asked, "Who am I?" I mouthed his name, but no words came out. Although I realized I was in the hospital room, I did not immediately remember why. Because the fire compromised my vision, and I was wearing protective goggles, my other senses seemed to be heightened. I could hear the steady beeping of the IV machine next to me. I could smell the sterile medical smells that filled the hospital corridors. My hospital gown had a unique scent that I will never forget. My throat was extremely dry, parched beyond anything I had ever felt. I needed water, but more urgently, I needed to get out of there.

Even in a medically induced coma, I had a level of awareness. I knew I was in a dream state, but could not figure out how to wake up. I had recurring nightmares and hallucinations the whole time I was unconscious in the ICU. I believe this was because of a drug called Ketamine, a medication used for the induction and maintenance of anesthesia. Although FDA-approved as a general anesthetic, it is known to produce hallucinations. When I finally woke up, I was sure that the people around me were trying to hurt me or, even worse, kill me. My nightmares were torturous scenarios where I would be fighting for my life in one situation, only for another equally horrifying situation to begin immediately after the last one ended. No one in the hospital was trying to kill me, but in my mental state upon waking, I did not know that.

With my limited ability to communicate, I thought I could convey to my husband what I believed was happening, and he would get me out of that place.

I said, "Please take me home. They are going to kill me."

My husband looked concerned. "What are you trying to say?"

I tried to make my lips form every word very clearly and distinctly so that he could at least read my lips if he could not hear me. "Take me home, or I will die!"

My husband called over to the nurse in the room, who was focused on other tasks. "Ma'am, she is trying to talk, but I don't understand what she is trying to say."

The nurse came to my bedside, and I immediately stopped

trying to speak. In my mind, she was the enemy and one of the people who had been torturing me. She was an excellent nurse, and my assumption was far from the truth. However, in my confusion, I truly believed she would hurt me. I did not want her to become aware of my plan to escape. Eventually, she left the room, and I was alone with my husband again.

I got his attention and made a gesture with my burned and bandaged hands as if I was writing with a pen and paper. Visiting hours were over, and my husband understood the gesture, so he stated he would bring me a pen and paper tomorrow so I could write what I was trying to say. I allowed my head to relax back against the pillow and roll down towards my shoulder. I was tremendously frustrated. I had things I wanted to say, but no way to express them. I was afraid, confused, and physically exhausted.

The next day, my husband returned with a pen and paper. He put the pen in my disfigured hand and held the paper in front of me. I was so excited because I could finally tell him what they had been doing to me, and he would take me home. I proceeded to write, "HELP ME. THEY ARE GOING TO KILL ME!" As I tried to form the first letter, I realized that although my mind knew how to write the letter, my hand would not follow the command. I could not write! I started panicking a little because I could not believe this was happening. I tried again to write another letter, and the same thing happened: My hand could not draw the letter. I felt so frustrated. I could not talk, nor could I write. I could not communicate at all. My thoughts were trapped in my mind, and I immediately felt hopeless.

My husband comforted me: "Don't worry. Just relax and rest." But I did not want to relax or rest; I wanted him to get me out of there. Most of the nurses were fantastic, and my fear was simply an irrational side effect of the nightmares I had experienced. I wanted to go home because I had no idea how bad my injuries were. I had not seen them and was not paying attention to all my bandages. It would not be until I went for my first shower in the hospital that I would come to full knowledge of what had happened to me and the extent of damage the fire and boiling hot oil caused to my body.

Showers were extremely painful, but necessary for wound healing and mitigating infections. However, removing bandages that were literally stuck to healing wounds felt as if the nurses were ripping off the top layer of my skin. The pain was harrowing enough to cause me to shake and shiver with fear whenever I knew they were coming to get me for my daily shower. The very first shower I received while fully conscious gave me a glimpse at my burned body. What I saw was unbelievable! How could an accident that happened in a split second cause so much damage? That marked the beginning of a deep and difficult depression.

The pain of second- and third-degree burns was intense, unrelenting, and enough to make me wish that God would have just taken me rather than spared my life. You probably know how painful burns can be if you have ever burned your hand in the hot oven or burned your finger on a curling iron. Think of that pain spread over a huge surface area of a person's body. There are no adequate words to describe it. Many days, I wondered why God did not just allow me to die. Every day in the hospital was mentally overwhelming. I was fed through a nasogastric tube, which carried food to my stomach through my nose, and given pain medications intravenously. I could not talk or eat, and I could barely walk.

Eventually, the doctors removed my nasogastric tube, but after not eating for weeks, I had no appetite or desire to chew food. The nurses noticed this and playfully threatened that they would put the NG tube back in if I did not eat. I hated this idea because nothing was more uncomfortable than laying in bed severely burned with multiple lines and tubes attached to or coming out of different parts of my body. I would stare at my plate of food with thoughts of dumping it in the trash and covering the evidence with napkins because it was so difficult to eat. It was not as simple as putting the food in my mouth and chewing it; I just could not physically eat more than a few bites. Slowly, one meal at a time, I made progress.

Progress on my road to recovery came in many forms. The

respiratory therapist gave me a cap for my tracheostomy, which allowed me to talk in a robotic voice. I appreciated the ability to communicate, although the cap was not an entirely positive experience. When I would try to walk, even the short distance from my bed to the restroom, breathing around the capped tracheostomy felt like the equivalent of breathing through a straw. I felt like I did not have enough air. On numerous occasions, when I finally reached the restroom, I broke out in a complete panic attack. With my hospital gown intertwined with my IV pole and lines, I would search for the nurse call button in the restroom.

One particular time, I paged the nurse and mustered up just enough air to form the words, "Help. I cannot breathe." The nurse rushed into the bathroom. Upon realizing that I was having a full-blown panic attack, she stooped down to my level, looked me in the eyes, and said, "Breathe. Breathe, sweetheart. You are fine." I took long, slow breaths as the disdain for that tracheostomy built in my mind. I wanted it out so much that I imagined pulling it out of my neck, but I knew that would only make matters worse. There was a breathing test that I was required to pass to remove the tracheostomy that measured my ability to breathe on my own. Each time I failed it, I held back tears. Eventually, my respiratory therapist felt my breathing was strong enough to remove it. I remember that was one of the best days of my time in the hospital.

Home Not-So-Sweet Home

Returning home was the scariest experience ever. The care I received in the hospital required a highly skilled team of doctors, nurses, physical therapists, and a psychiatrist. At home, my husband would somehow have to fill all those roles, in addition to working a full-time job and being a parent. That was a lot for one person to manage, and I was worried about his mental health. My husband had no medical experience except the techniques the hospital staff showed him to care for me. He was confident in his ability to care for my needs, but I was so afraid. I felt the cloak of depression slowly becoming heavier and heavier. The hospital, although frustrating sometimes, felt like a safe place for me after I understood no one was trying to harm me.

My husband became my caregiver, and I became embarrassed and resentful of my situation. My care required an almost two-hour process of unbandaging me, bathing me, removing any loose skin or scabs, putting on my medicated ointments and creams, and rebandaging me. I was completely reliant on my husband and could barely do anything for myself. The most debilitating body parts were my burned hands because it hurt tremendously to use them. Any friction caused immense pain and damage to the healing skin. I wanted nothing more than to take care of myself, my children, and my household, but this was impossible. I was very independent before my accident, but now, I felt utterly useless. This feeling attacked my self-worth. Long therapy discussions helped me appreciate the small victories in my abilities at different points along my healing journey.

I experienced very intense dreams after the accident. They were vivid dreams of me in my pre-accident condition—smooth skin, no burns, and no pain. In my dreams, I would be so happy, doing an activity that I enjoyed. It was the most blissful state. However, a wave of grief would hit me like a boulder when I woke up. Before I could fully open my eyes, I would feel intense pain. The immediate feeling of pain shocked me out of a joyful dream state and back into the nightmare that was my reality. Each morning, I was greeted with the harsh realization that my accident had really happened and that I no longer looked the way I did in my dreams. This truth left me so disappointed, and sadness set the tone for the rest of the day.

I wanted nothing more than for the accident not to be real. I wished I could have woken up to all I had experienced the last few months having never happened so my life could return to normal. But, of course, this never happened. I cannot describe the depths of mental anguish I felt each time I woke up and realized I was in this battle for my life and my sanity once again! I cried warm, intense tears many mornings upon waking, and it took several months for those dreams of me in my pre-accident state to go away. I guess my mind had to catch up with my body.

I continued a practice I had started in the hospital of reading books, watching videos, and viewing social media pages of other burn survivors as a source of hope and inspiration. I felt no one could fully understand what I was going through except other burn survivors. Years after their accidents, they were living the most beautiful lives. This let me know happiness was possible; I just needed to figure out how to get there from where I was. I consumed everything I could find online and absorbed as much positivity from their lives as possible. I am so thankful that those burn survivors decided to share their stories with the world because they were an integral part of why I am here today, even though they will likely never know it.

A Diary Entry

This is an actual journal entry written a few months after returning home from the hospital.

Today is July 12, 2019. I have just woken up from a nap . The truth is, at 6:20 p.m., I have not gotten out of bed all day except to use the restroom and grab a drink. Even in those moments, I quickly ran back to the comfort of my bed as soon as possible. Another truth is I feel depressed. This depression is not fueled so much by how I look, but rather by how I feel. My body feels horrible! I will try my best to describe what it feels like approximately four months after the fire destroyed my life and took away the motivation that pushed me to set the highest personal goals for myself.

The worst parts of me are my hands. They hurt every day as thick, hard, contracted scar tissue covers six of my fingers. Two of those fingers do not bend, preventing me from closing my left hand. My hands tingle, ache, throb, and feel heightened pain upon contact with everyday objects. This feeling does not come and go, but instead is constant. I have always had a high pain tolerance, so the sensation in my hands is a bit more tolerable than the itching I experience twenty-four hours a day. The itching is making me lose my mind.

My donor sites, where doctors harvested skin to use over

my burned areas, itch with unbearable intensity all day and night. The itching has caused me to scratch my back and hip until they bled. It has caused me to scream and cry to the top of my lungs and squirm on my floor in a snake-like motion to scratch the huge donor site on my back while declaring, "I cannot take this anymore!" The doctors have prescribed three anti-itch medications to take in conjunction with one another, and none have worked. I have thought many times to myself that I would rather be in pain than feel constant itching. The itching keeps me from going grocery shopping, going to church, or doing other daily life activities out of fear that I will be unbearably uncomfortable. I will have laser surgery in two weeks, which is supposed to calm the itchy areas by targeting the nerves that are going crazy as they grow back.

Lastly, the parts of my body where scars are thickening, like across my chest and along my rib cage, offer no stretch or flexibility for things like rolling out of bed or sitting up. Because of this, when I try to do those things, I have to slowly take my time to avoid a ripping sensation of the skin in those areas. Even with slow movement, I can feel contracted skin stretching beyond its limits, giving me the feeling that the skin is ripping.

My husband is in the kitchen cooking dinner as I type this. I have not cooked a single thing since my accident in March. I am afraid of the stove or anything that can burn me, and I am not ready to push past that mental trauma. The way my body feels daily leaves me feeling hopeless, helpless, worthless, and even disappointed in myself that I don't push past those feelings of discomfort to accomplish some of my duties as a wife and mother.

A heavy blanket of sadness covered me when I woke up from my nap. It was thick and palpable and interwoven with feelings of fear that a person would typically experience when waking up from a nightmare. I also felt the "panic attack" emotions well inside me. I know those feelings all too well, as I have had many panic attacks over the past few months. My mind began racing from one negative thought to another: You are never going to be your old self. Your body will always feel this horrible. You will always be limited from doing the things you used to do. You will never be beautiful again. You might as well give up on life.

As each negative thought entered my mind, I tried to counter it with a positive one so I would not have a panic attack. I was able to calm myself down; however, I don't feel happy at the point that I am writing this. I cannot see the light at the end of the tunnel. Burns are so complicated, and the healing process is lengthy. As my wounds heal, scar tissue makes me feel like I'm not making progress, but rather stuck in a place that is neither moving forward nor backward.

With all this being said, I will not be defeated. No one will ever say that Ebonee was burned and never recovered from her injuries mentally or physically. I go to rehab every day with courageous burn survivors who have 50%, 60%, and 70% of their bodies burned, but are making great strides with smiles on their faces. They have lost fingers, limbs, the face they once knew, and so much more, yet are rising above these challenges. I love each and every one of the burn survivors I meet. I love them because they understand my pain, and I understand theirs. I feel as if they are almost my brothers. I have not met one woman burn survivor in the outpatient clinic. I would love to meet other women because I would be able to relate to them more. Most women care about their appearance just as much as I do—we take pride in looking and feeling our best.

Burns can completely destroy your self-image if you let them, and I am scarred from head to toe! Regardless of this, I told myself early on that I would love my body and never hide my scars. This is still my plan as I fight to regain a sense of who I am physically, on the outside. I know who I am on the inside. I am writing this on a day when my emotions feel very low. Hopefully, a few months into the future, I will be able to say that this time in my life was just a small challenge that I overcame, and I became stronger for it.

Physical Therapy & Psychological Support

Similar to how I felt in the hospital, physical therapy felt like a safe place for me. I felt a connection to the other burn survivors there. We all had the same struggles and were all trying to get better, though it was tough. I encountered people with burns that were less severe than mine, and others had injuries significantly worse. There was a young guy in his early twenties who had burns so severe he had to have his legs amputated from the knee down. Another courageous young man jumped from a burning building to save his life and was missing a portion of his skull from landing on his head.

I wanted to know everyone's stories, especially those who were further along in their recovery than me. Those encouraging conversations gave me hope that was the equivalent of food for my soul. One burn survivor would say, "Trust me, it gets better. I promise." Another would say, "Try this cream for your itching; it helped me a lot when I was four months into recovery like you are." I could feel a palpable strength in the physical therapy area. This developed my love for the burn survivor community. I would see people fighting so hard to rebuild their lives. I wanted to fight, too. I really wanted to be happy again.

Even though physical therapy felt like a safe place for me, many days I waited in the waiting room for my therapist to call me back on the verge of a complete breakdown. One day, a sweet therapist greeted me in the waiting room. She was a beautiful brown-complected, thirty-something-year-old woman with a Haitian accent. She always greeted me like I was an old friend. She had a big spirit in her petite body. Before she could even ask me how I was doing that day, I broke down in tears. I could not even speak; the words would not form in my mouth. She understood my inability to communicate and simply said, "Let's take a walk today." We walked down the hospital corridors and stopped next to a big bright window, and she asked me again, "What is wrong today, Ebonee?" I still could not verbalize why I was crying.

It was built-up mental pain that had reached the surface from trying to be strong for too long. Like bubbling lava spewing from a volcano, my emotions erupted from the inside out. I was struggling to accept my appearance. My face was crusted with scabs and pink healing wounds. Most days, I could not bear to look in the mirror, but somehow had to muster up the courage to go out in public. I pulled out my phone and pulled up my Instagram page. I showed her the picture I took on the same day of the accident before I was burned.

I handed her the phone and said, "Do you see this?"

She said, "Yes, I see it. And what?"

I was confused at her response. I was expecting a different reaction. I expected her to say, "Wow, that is a beautiful picture."

She continued to explain that superficial things did not make me Ebonee and that I was more than my appearance. She expressed that the person I was had not changed and that I needed to stop being so concerned with how I looked. Her tone was a balance of care and firmness. I immediately felt grateful for her delivery because, for some reason, it gave me the freedom to let go of this image of myself I was holding on to so tightly. This version of myself that I would never see again was causing me so much sadness. She convinced me that I had to start looking at myself for who I was on the inside, the part of me unchanged after the accident. She confirmed that I was still in there, still inside this burned body, and the qualities that made me unique and special were still there.

This conversation opened a new perspective for me. Was I, in fact, still the same person? For many years, so much of my identity was wrapped up in how I looked. I was a woman who loved make-up and changing my hair into many beautiful hairstyles. I also loved clothes and accessories. I was always striving to be the perfect weight. My appearance was a large part of who I knew myself to be. I would have never admitted it then, but there was probably a level of vanity to it as well. To be stripped of my face and the beautiful even brown skin tone on my body in the blink of an eye was unfathomably traumatic and caused much psychological distress. My appearance and future scars deeply saddened me. Although the pain and itching were unbearable, and the recovery process was long and frustrating, these things would go away one day. However, I knew that the scars would never go away. I would be scarred for life! It wasn't easy to come to terms with that.

On another occasion, I came to physical therapy and got on the stationary bike for my warm-up. As I was pedaling, people passed me by, greeting me with variations of "Good morning." I tried to put on a slight smile and respond, but I was so sad inside. The sadness was so immense that it affected my ability to walk and even lift my head or move my face. I felt as if this sadness made me do everything in slow motion. Looking back, I now know I was battling depression. On that particular day, I guess others could tell I was depressed because I had two therapists approach me while I was warming up to inquire about my mental state. Their questions led me to say, "I don't want to be here anymore."

One therapist attempted to clarify my response with another question. "Do you mean you want to go home?"

"No," I said. "I don't want to live anymore. It is too hard."

I could see the alarm on the therapists' faces. They tried to remain calm for my sake, but I know they were trained to report any potential suicidal statements so the patient could get mental health support that they were not qualified to give in the physical therapy department. I sat there, numb. Even though I said exactly how I felt, I did not want anyone to convince me not to commit suicide.

A few days prior, I had experienced suicidal thoughts while sitting in the parking lot of my son's daycare. The only number I felt comfortable calling was one of those 1-800 suicide prevention and crisis hotlines. When I got the representative on the line, she had a calm and caring voice and inquired about my current situation. As I began to pour out my emotions, I immediately noticed she was not listening to me. I heard some side conversations in the background, and I asked her if she had heard anything I said. She responded, "I am sorry you feel this way," which I realized was a canned response she was trained to say. She truly was not listening and probably did not care. I disconnected the line and felt so sad that even a hotline dedicated to suicide prevention did care about what I was experiencing.

I had multiple orange and white bottles of pain medications, anti-itch prescriptions, and antI-depressants sitting on my nightstand. Many days, I thought about opening each bottle and taking every single pill to overdose and end my suffering. I absolutely and unconditionally love my children, but I had convinced myself that, in my condition, I was not a mother to them. Many days, I would miss my physical therapy sessions and never even get out of bed. My negative thoughts would justify committing suicide by telling me my kids would be okay if I were no longer here because I was in the bed all day anyway.

On those days, I would cry out to God—many times without words, just with tears and emotions. "Likewise the Spirit helps us in our weakness. For we do not know what to pray for as we ought, but the Spirit himself intercedes for us with groanings too deep for words" (Romans 8:26). Sometimes, all I could pray was, "Help me, please." The suicidal thoughts would pass, and I would live to battle them another day.

Reflecting back to the day at physical therapy, when I informed the therapists that I did not want to live, the psychologist assigned to support all the burn survivors was unavailable, as he was a very busy man meeting with both inpatient and outpatient burn survivors. Because it was a military hospital, the staff located the chaplain to speak with me as a secondary support option. The chaplain entered the room I was sitting in with positive energy radiating from his whole body. He was a Caucasian man, looked to be in his mid-fifties, around six feet tall, and donned in an Army combat uniform. He was in such a good mood that day that it was hard for me to remain in such a low state while in his presence. This is the power of having an uplifting and positive personality—people around you benefit, too.

Although I don't remember everything he said, I remember our discussion made me understand the value of my life. He expressed that I was important and strong enough to overcome this situation. He shared that I had so much more living to do and gave me examples of things I may be missing out on by not continuing to fight for my life. The thing the chaplain gave me that day was hope—hope that better days are ahead if I can just hold on. Hope is a powerful thing. I never hesitate to give another person hope in what seems to be a hopeless situation. When I left physical therapy that day, I was still very depressed, but I was resolute that suicide was not a solution. Every day that passed was one day closer to happier days.

God's Healing & My Purpose

Healing did not come through one person or thing, but a combination of many. God completely healed me and used many friends, family members, doctors, therapists, books, videos, situations, and revelations to do this. Today, I have no medical problems and take no medications. I no longer battle depression. In fact, I am the happiest I have ever been and have an infectiously optimistic perspective on life. However, it was a process to get to the place I am today.

Many days, I questioned why God would allow me to experience something so traumatic. Although I know that everyone will experience challenges in their lives, I felt becoming a burn survivor was a severely cruel and unfair thing to go through. I searched my life to determine if I was *deserving* of such a fate. I asked, "God, if You love me, why would You allow me to experience so much pain?" Many days, this was my conversation with God. However, my thought process was all wrong. It wasn't about whether I deserved my fate, but the lessons I should be learning from this and the lives I would impact.

I always felt God telling me in a very gentle and empathetic way, "This is something you must experience for the lessons you need to learn." I also felt Him telling me that so much good would come out of this situation. Just like Romans 8:28 states, "All things work together for good to those who love God, to those who are the called according to *His* purpose." I struggled with that truth. Some days as I was healing, the pain and itching of my body were too much to bear. I only had the energy to say, "God, help me, please." I would say it over and over. I would take comfort in the fact that God heard me, and eventually, a peace would wash over me that allowed me to either close my eyes and sleep or refocus my attention on something other than pain. In those moments of crying out to God, the relief almost felt like a spiritual hug. I felt wrapped in love, comfort, and care. I do not doubt that what I was experiencing was directly from God as a loving response to my cries.

My body continued to heal over time—open wounds closed, and thick scars softened and flattened. My sensitive skin slowly began to feel normal. The flexibility returned to my hands, and I could use them for more and more things. I could bend my fingers that were previously stuck in place. I could braid hair again! This was something that I had done since I was a little girl, but that I feared I would never be able to do again with my hands.

The more I healed, the more I felt an enormous urge to help others heal. I did not want anyone to suffer the way I did for longer than necessary. Although physical pain and limitations are absolutely real, I learned that much suffering is mental and can be alleviated with mindset shifts. Sometimes, we suffer longer than necessary because we look at our situation from the perspective of "Why did this happen to me?" rather than "What can I learn from this?" God immediately started putting people and opportunities in my path for me to share my story and show compassion and understanding to those currently suffering. I felt the connections were divine and part of my life's purpose.

I know my suffering was not in vain. I can connect with others on a deeper level than ever before because of my experiences. I understand pain because I have felt pain profoundly and intensely. I know depression because I battled it with every ounce of my existence. I am able to empathize with anxiety, PTSD, and panic attacks because they were my daily companions for months.

I know what it feels like to be stripped of self-esteem, confidence, and self-worth due to scars and visible differences, and I now see the beauty in people that resonates from within, deeper than surface level. I want people living with scars to know their beauty, so I use my social media pages as a blogger and content creator to highlight the lessons my accident has taught me and is still teaching me. One major lesson is unconditional self-love.

It makes me feel good to help others as a result of becoming a burn survivor. God sends confirmation through various people, letting me know that I am walking in my purpose and doing good work to bring light to this Earth. It is gratifying and immensely rewarding, so much so that I would not change what I have been through if I had the opportunity to go back in time. The burn accident was a necessary part of my evolution and spiritual growth. It is an essential part of the person I am today. I now know why God allowed it to happen. He knew what the other side of this accident would look like for me and the people connected to me.

A pastor once told me, "Ebonee, think about how many people's destinies are connected to your life. If you give up now, God will have to find someone else to fill the role He meant for you." That was powerful because even if I did not have the strength to continue for myself, I imagined the hundreds or thousands of people who would benefit from my life. I did not want to let them down. I am here because God healed me, and I also have the privilege of helping others heal.

Ebonee Debrah

Chapter 2
Shaken but Still Winning

Shortly after two knocks on the driver-side window of my vehicle, a police officer raised his voice and said, "Ma'am, you're on top of a fire hydrant. Yes, your car is on top of a fire hydrant."

Initially, I didn't have the slightest clue of what he was talking about. With a bad attitude, I replied, "What?" Then, he asked me if I had been drinking alcohol and was possibly drunk. I told him I had not had any alcoholic beverages that evening. He proceeded and asked me to get out of the car. Eventually, I complied, and sure enough, the front passenger side of my car was on top of a fire hydrant. In spite of me assuring the officer that I had not drank any liquor that night, he still administered a sobriety test. As I knew I would, I went on to pass the test. Upon completion of the officer checking my sobriety, I let him know that I battled with epilepsy, and I believed I had an episode while driving home.

This all occurred one summer evening in 2014 on Highway 90 in Avondale, Louisiana, which is on the Westbank of New Orleans. To this day, whenever I pass that area, I always thank God for the fire hydrant because if it had not been there, I would have driven into a ditch or someone's home. I thank God because instead of the evening ending with my uncle and boyfriend working together to get my car from on top of the hydrant, it could have ended with a much worse scenario. Although my battle with epilepsy began six years prior to that night, I'd never experienced a seizure while behind the wheel.

Seizures randomly began in my life in 2008 while I was visiting Atlanta, Georgia. A wonderful sorority sister of mine gladly opened her home for me to stay during my visit, and one morning, I woke up on a bloody pillow with a swollen tongue. Seeing the blood and feeling the teeth prints on my tongue was truly confusing because I did not feel the severe tongue bite during my sleep. It didn't make any sense to me how something so severe could happen, but I had absolutely no recollection of it happening. The pain from the bitten tongue was nearly unbearable, and I could barely speak due to the extreme swelling of my tongue. However, in spite of the confusion and pain, I managed to enjoy the remainder of my trip to the best of my ability.

When I returned home to Avondale, Louisiana, I shared the experience with my family. Of course, they were all just as confused as I was about what could have possibly occurred while I was asleep. As the days passed and my tongue healed, I shrugged the incident off as something that simply *just happened.* Over the next month and a half, there were at least two more times when I woke up with a swollen tongue on a bloody pillow.

After the second time, my mother said, "Ashley, maybe you are having those things."

I didn't know what things she was referring to, so I questioned, "What things, Ma?"

She replied, "You know those things, seizures."

Immediately, I denied having seizures because I couldn't understand how or why I would randomly begin experiencing seizures at the age of twenty-two.

It wasn't until one day when my cousin and I were taking a nap in the same bed that it became clear what I had been experiencing. She said my body began to shake and she told me to stop; however, my body continued to shake, and I was unresponsive. Then, she yelled for the family to come into the room and see what was happening. When my grandmother saw me, she said, "That girl is having a seizure." They were all very terrified by what they were seeing me go through and immediately called 911.

As the paramedics were on their way, my family began to do things that they thought were correct to do for someone experiencing a seizure. They put a spoon in my mouth because they'd heard the old saying that a person experiencing a seizure can swallow their tongue. My family members worked together to get me out of the bed and bring me into the living room. The ambulance arrived, and the paramedics rushed me to the emergency room.

While on the way to the emergency room, I began to regain consciousness. The paramedics explained that we were on our way to the emergency room. After arriving at the hospital, the ER nurses performed various tests and asked me multiple questions about my medical history, my parents' medical background, and if I ever had trauma to my head. Following the series of tests and questions, the medical team told me that I had suffered a nocturnal seizure, which is a seizure that occurs while asleep. I was in total disbelief because I didn't understand how, at the age of twenty-two, I would start having seizures without any previous head trauma or family history of the disorder.

Not long after my visit to the emergency room, I scheduled appointments to see a neurologist. I wanted to get a better understanding of what was going on within my body. I spoke with the neurologist, and he suggested that I have a brain scan done to check the activity on my brain. I was compliant with him and scheduled a twelve-hour-long test that would possibly give answers to what was going on inside of me. Once the test was complete, the doctor couldn't give a reason why or how I started experiencing the seizures, but he diagnosed me with the incurable disorder of epilepsy.

Over the next fourteen years, I experienced multiple types of seizures, and they had different effects on me. The seizures mainly affected me physically and emotionally. The physical effects included severe headaches, tongue bites, and injuries from falls, along with others. Although it may have taken days or even weeks for me to recuperate from the physical effects, the emotional effects lasted much longer and had an overall larger impact on my life.

The emotional effects of me having a seizure were not only on myself, but also those around me. It was never easy for a family member or friend to experience me having a seizure. Unfortunately, whenever they saw my body go through the changes of a seizure, they knew there wasn't much they could do to help me, and there wasn't anything they could do to stop the seizure. The most important thing that anyone could do while I was going through a seizure was to make sure that I didn't hurt myself by falling or hitting my head. The overall feeling of helplessness saddened those around me because they really wished there was more they could do to help me throughout such a trying time.

Epilepsy includes various types of seizures. Absence seizures along with tonic-clonic seizures were the most prevalent during my battle with the disorder. Both of these seizure types fall into the group of generalized seizures. This group of seizures had an effect on both sides of my brain and could be experienced while awake or asleep.

Absence seizures, also known as petit mal seizures, caused me to lose consciousness and stare into space for periods of time. There were times when I was in the middle of a conversation and then began to randomly stare for up to twelve minutes. Other times, I may have gone from speaking clearly to speaking with a slur and eventually not speaking at all. While staring, I was unaware of everything going on around me. After multiple minutes of no consciousness and staring, I would slowly begin to come back to myself. Even though the staring would end and I would start coming back to myself after a few minutes, it could take me days to fully feel like myself again.

Regardless of the seizure type, a seizure was never an easy experience. However, the scariest and most dangerous of them all are tonic-clonic seizures, also known as grand mal seizures. This type of seizure has happened while I was awake and even during my sleep. It was the scariest and most dangerous because along with losing total consciousness, my body would go into convulsions.

Grand mal seizures were the most dangerous because of uncontrolled convulsions. During the convulsions, my body would tense up, I'd begin to shake, and then I'd lose full control of my body. I would not have any idea of what was going on while these activities were taking place because all of my consciousness would be gone. The convulsions would be so strong that after

32

coming out of a grand mal seizure, I felt like I'd just completed an extensive full-body workout. It was also during this form of seizure that I'd bite my tongue because even the muscles in my face would tense up.

While having grand mal seizures, I've fell multiple times and seriously injured myself. For example, two days before my bridal shower, which was a week before my wedding, I fell during a grand mal episode and hit my head on the corner of a dresser. Thankfully, I was in the room with one of my cousins, and she heard me fall. When she looked, I was on the floor in a river of blood that was running from above my left eye. She was extremely terrified and shouted for our cousin, who was in another room, to come help. They called the paramedics, but as I was going in and out of consciousness, I told them that I did not want to go to the hospital. At that point, I did not know the severity of the injury. They insisted on calming me down and told me that I didn't have any other choice but to go to the hospital.

While on the way to the hospital, I told the paramedics that I just wanted to talk to my fiancé. After constantly telling them that I wanted to speak with him, one of the paramedics used their personal cell phone to call him. It was in the wee hours of the night, but he answered the phone. I told him that I was in an ambulance on my way to the hospital because of a seizure. He was worried because he was hundreds of miles away and couldn't be there with me. Before getting off the phone, he told me that he loved me and asked me to keep him posted on everything that happened in the ER.

My cousins and other family members arrived at the emergency room not long after I was admitted. This occurred right before COVID-19 was declared a pandemic, so only one family member could come into my room. By that time, my mother had made it to the hospital, and when she walked into my room, she was in total disbelief at the injury she saw on my forehead. I asked her to take a picture on her phone so I could see the injury. It wasn't until then that I saw the severity of the injury, and all I could do was simply thank God for protecting my life and keeping me alive.

While in the emergency room, I received twenty-one stitches above my left eye. A couple days later, I went to my bridal shower stitched up and with a black eye, but I still had a smile on my face. Even though the major injury had taken place, I was truly thankful for the breath flowing in and out of my body. In spite of having more than twenty stitches over my eye, I had faith that I would still look beautiful on my wedding day, and thank God I did.

The fourteen-year journey I was on with seizures was definitely a confusing one because doctors across multiple states were never able to explain why seizures began to attack my body. Medical professionals in Louisiana, California, and Georgia have ordered many different types of brain scans to search for the possible cause of the disorder, but were never been able to pinpoint the root of epilepsy. They also conducted brain scans during my sleep to detect any epileptic activity in my brain. None of the brain scans ordered by any of the professionals ever showed any type of epileptic activity on my brain. The fact that epileptic activity never showed up allowed me to remain faithful that this disorder was not something that *I ever had*; however, it was a disorder that I was in a *battle* with, and with God's healing power, I would win the battle.

Along with the multiple brain scans, doctors prescribed me a variety of medications in various dosages to try to combat seizures. Unfortunately, they were never able to come up with a prescription that totally stops the seizures. I was never 100% seizure-free while taking the various medicines. Although I hadn't been completely free of seizures, there were times when the number of episodes was lower than other times.

Because I took the seizure medication for such a long period of time, it impacted my life in various ways. One of the main impacts it had was the loss of my memory—mainly, my short-term memory. At first, I didn't realize that I was losing my memory. I began to notice that parts of my memory were slipping away one evening while I was driving around downtown New Orleans. During my drive, I started thinking about the thirty-one women I went through the process of joining my beloved sorority with, but I couldn't remember the name we had chosen for our line. I struggled to find the name in my memory bank, but "The 32 Triumphant Trailblazers of Tribulation" would not come to my memory. When I recognized that I couldn't think of our line name, I pulled my car over and began to cry. I was embarrassed, and it hurt me so much to know that I couldn't remember something that I held so close to my heart.

Over time, my memory loss started becoming more obvious to people around me. During a general conversation, someone would ask, "Do you remember when…?" My reply would be, "No, I don't remember." They would question how I could not remember what they were talking about. Then, they'd say that it hadn't been too long since the situation occurred. I began to have to explain to those around me how the seizure medication was affecting my memory.

Although it became more and more obvious that certain parts of my memory were diminishing, one thing that I never liked was whenever someone would remind me that I couldn't remember things. What I mean by that is if someone started a conversation by saying, "I know you are not going to remember this, but…," that statement always irked me because I never needed to be reminded of the issues I was having with my memory. Even though I knew the person didn't mean to offend me with the statement, I still felt offended and hurt.

Because I was in denial of my battle with seizures when it first started, it took a while before I began to pay attention to the things that were causing the epileptic episodes, which are called triggers. One of my main triggers was alcoholic beverages. At the very beginning of my battle with seizures, doctors informed me that alcoholic beverages did not mix well with epilepsy medications and could cause severe seizures. They also told me that alcohol could increase the occurrence of seizures. In spite of being given this information, I still drank alcohol, and sure enough, it resulted in many severe seizures.

Another main trigger for me was certain foods and drinks. All throughout my life, I loved various seafoods (e.g. shrimp and blue crabs). It wasn't until years after my battle with seizures began that I noticed how these particular seafoods were triggers.

Whenever I ate shrimp, blue crabs, or dishes made with either of the two, there was a high possibility that I would have a seizure. Obviously, I loved the taste of the foods, but in no way did I love the effect they had on my body.

Highly caffeinated drinks like coffee, lattes, cappuccinos, mochas, and energy drinks would also cause seizures. I typically drank these drinks simply for their taste because I rarely felt any boost of energy from them. Although I couldn't feel any changes in my energy, these drinks would increase the nerve cell activity in my brain. The increased brain activity would cause me to have seizures.

Other triggers included stress, not getting enough rest, and even my monthly menstrual cycle. It took many years for me to pinpoint the triggers. As time went on, I knew and was able to pinpoint the triggers which included stress, inadequate rest, and my menstrual cycle. As time went on, I was able to recognize the triggers, I asked myself, *What good is it to have faith and know the things that you need to do, but still not do them?* This question came to me one day while reading James 2:17: "Thus also faith by itself, if it does not have works, is dead." I always had faith that God would heal me of the disorder; however, I wasn't putting in the work that needed to be done in order for me to be healed. I reflected on instances when I was inconsistent with taking medications, ate certain foods, drank highly caffeinated drinks, or drank alcohol, and those were the times when I was not working toward my healing.

After looking back on times when I was not working, I knew I had to make some lifestyle alterations in order to try to slow down and end the seizures. Although I was not able to make all of the changes overnight, I eventually made the necessary changes. For example, a couple of months following me having the twenty-one stitches above my eye, I had a drink for a friend's birthday. That evening, I had a seizure while asleep, which resulted in me falling out of the bed and getting a carpet burn on my face.

The next morning, when I woke up on the floor and saw the burn, I told myself that I was done with alcohol. That decision was made when I looked at the severity of the recent injuries I'd endured and considered how much worse they could have turned out. I even thought about how God had given me multiple opportunities to continue on with life. While contemplating these things, I had to stop and question myself: Is having a drink worth your life? God keeps giving you opportunities in life. Why are you taking them for granted? How many opportunities do you expect Him to give you? At that point, I told myself that I was done with drinking alcohol, and following that day, I never had another drink that contained alcohol.

There was a time when I was truly stressed out because I didn't know where my career was going. I had jobs in different industries, but none of them felt right for me. The stress was causing me to have seizures while on the job. At times, it was truly embarrassing to come back to my consciousness and see coworkers standing around me, wondering if I was okay. I hated the negative impact that the seizures would have on my coworkers and the overall work environment.

After lots of prayer and discussion with family members, I decided to take some time off from work. Although I knew this was the best decision that I could make at that time, it still caused some depression. Whenever I'd think about my years spent in undergraduate and graduate college and how seizures were forcing me to stay home, it would have a negative mental impact on me. The decision was not only made because of the stress my career path was causing, but also because I experienced another seizure while driving.

This time, I was driving in the daytime on a busy highway in New Orleans. Thank God, I was not in the car alone, but my boyfriend was with me. When he looked over and saw me going into a seizure, he immediately put the car in park and turned on the hazard lights. He got out of the passenger seat and ran to the driver's side to get me out of the driver's seat.

I never wanted to be considered disabled; I looked at myself as just someone who was in a battle with a disorder. The feeling of depression really set in when I had to humble myself and apply for Social Security Disability to help with my monthly expenses. The simple thought of receiving a disability check didn't sit well with me. After applications and appeals, I was eventually approved for monetary government assistance. I made a vow to myself that I would never get comfortable accepting Social Security assistance. I told myself that I would make changes in my lifestyle so that one day, I would be 100% seizure-free and able to handle working a job without the fear of epileptic episodes attacking me.

So many times in my life, the enemy tried his hardest to get me to let go of my faith. However, time and time again, I had to show him that he would never prevail. Leading up to, and even during, the time I was writing the very words you're reading, my body was being attacked by countless nocturnal seizures. The episodes were surprising because they came at a time in my life when doctors predicted that the seizures would actually slow down. In spite of it all, I told myself to hold on to my faith for several reasons, the main reason being that I knew God as Jehovah-Rapha, the Healer, and my trust in Him never waivered. He showed me several times that He would always cover, protect, and heal me from the unclean epileptic spirit.

While experiencing the increased seizures, I often wondered, *Why am I being attacked?* After spending time with God, He spoke to me and let me know that He wouldn't put more on me than I could bear. God also told me that the devil knew that my battle with seizures was coming to an end, so he was going to constantly test me to see if I would give up on God. During a conversation with God, He reminded me that my battle with the disorder began with nocturnal seizures, which are the seizures that occur during my sleep. He told me that the same way seizures came into my life many years ago, which was in the form of nocturnal seizures, was the same way they would leave my life. Additionally, He encouraged me to solicit the prayers of those around me and to hold on to my faith because He could do all things and was going to remove seizures from my life.

During my battle with epilepsy, I often referenced back to the subject text of a sermon my pastor once preached, which was Luke 9:37–42 (NKJV):

38

"Now it happened on the next day, when they had come down from the mountain, that a great multitude met Him. Suddenly a man from the multitude cried out, saying, "Teacher, I implore You, look on my son, for he is my only child. And behold, a spirit seizes him, and he suddenly cries out; it convulses him so that he foams at the mouth; and it departs from him with great difficulty, bruising him. So I implored Your disciples to cast it out, but they could not." Then Jesus answered and said, "O faithless and perverse generation, how long shall I be with you and bear with you? Bring your son here." And as he was still coming, the demon threw him down and convulsed him. Then Jesus rebuked the unclean spirit, healed the child, and gave him back to his father."

During the sermon, my pastor expounded on the father's faith that his son would be healed. I remembered this text and sermon because it wasn't many days prior to hearing the message that I'd been attacked by a seizure. Hearing this message boosted my spirit and assured me that one day, I would be healed. I felt so relieved and free after hearing this message to the point that I began to dance during the service. I could not contain my seat; the Holy Spirit led me to dance and give thanks.

There are anti-seizure medications that help manage the epilepsy to the point where it barely interferes with an individual's life, but unfortunately, there are currently no man-made medications to cure the condition. I was devastated when I was initially diagnosed and told that no drugs could cure me of the disorder. The thought of my body having to endure the physical and mental impacts of epilepsy for the rest of my life did not sit well with me. When I was diagnosed, doctors also told me that there was a higher risk of my offspring developing the same disorder. At the time, I didn't have any children; however, I could not imagine my future children having to experience the calamity that seizures had caused me.

It took some time for me to accept that doctors would not be able to prescribe me a man-made drug that would relieve me of the struggles I had with epilepsy. Once I accepted that man could not do it for me, I prescribed myself the combination of

Prayer, Trust, and Faith as my medication. With this prescription, I knew I would not have to battle seizures for the rest of my life. I also knew and believed that the disorder would not be passed onto my offspring. I strongly proclaimed that this prescription would remove all forms of seizures from my body.

One of the most visual impacts seizures had on me was the convulsions and the shaking my body experienced during grand mal episodes. I expressed to myself that one day, I would be able to look back over the years and see how seizures impacted various parts of my life. While looking back, I would also be able to testify how with my prescription of Prayer, Trust, and Faith, the shaking caused by seizures no longer occurred because with God's help I'd won my battle with epilepsy. Ultimately, I, along with those around me, would be able to see that even though my life was shaken by seizures and their effects, I was still winning.

Ashley N. Williams

Chapter 3
Good Grief

"Go see your mom" was ringing in my ears all day.

Why?

"I urge you to see your mom. It's not looking good."

What do you mean?

I felt like everyone around me was speaking an entirely different language.

Still no real reply—well, it wasn't to me. Every single person who speaks to me about my mother, was putting on a façade. No one was telling me the whole truth.

What in the world is happening with my mom?

"Your mother doesn't have any brain activity."

Excuse me—come again?

I was eighteen at the time, still baffled that my mother had been in the hospital for the last month with severe migraines. So, are you trying to tell me that my mother is dying? ... "Go see your mother" could only mean things had turned for the worst. *I mean, but she was just okay. Yesterday she told me, "Merry Christmas."* I remember the day like it happened just yesterday; it was December 26ᵗʰ, 2006. I was standing by the washing machine. The house smelled of pine because my mother preferred a real tree during the holidays, and I could hear the television on. My baby brothers were playing, laughing, and screaming each other's names, and they didn't have a clue what had just happened to our mother.

My dad finally said, "Momma don't look good. It doesn't look good, Dre."

I still couldn't understand, for the life of me, how a person could go into the hospital and never return home. Like, brain surgery can't be that difficult; she wouldn't risk not being here for us.

Then, I began to see people's spirits breaking down.

I said, "They are losing faith."

I remember my grand-aunt praying, "Lord, stand in the gate for Nicole." I was praying five times as hard, "Lord, please save my momma. Lord, hear my call. Take me instead. The boys need her; my dad needs her. Lord, she tithes every week, even when she works on the weekend." I would be singing gospel songs that resonated with me to the top of my lungs, and tears would roll down my cheeks. "Lord, save my momma. She's too young to die."

And then, I made up my mind that she would be a miracle; that when she heard my voice when I stepped into the hospital room, grabbed her hands, and kissed her face, she was going to wake up. So, now, I was determined to get to the hospital to save my mom because I just might be her saving grace. She would surely feel my energy and wake up.

She can't be brain dead.

People wake up from comas all the time.

She's just waiting for me.

She's taking a brief intermission.

She will return shortly, folks. Keep the faith.

I recall telling my grandmother, "We have to keep the faith, Gramma." I'd been calling her that for years. However, people around me began to lose faith. No. That was not accepting reality; not to me, because the God I serve can move mountains. Anyhow, I finally arrived at the hospital. I was anxious to see her, and nervous that everything would be true.

I took the elevator up to her floor, and I saw friends of hers there. I'm not sure how so many people knew because my mom was a very private person. She would not have wanted anyone to see her in the state that she was in. I bypassed them and entered her room. She had compressions around her legs. She had a deep, dark purple on her toenails and a bright reddish-orange Afro; I can't recall if it was braided or not. I scanned her up and down. I finally looked over, and my uncle Vander was there holding her hand, rubbing down her arm. He was this beautiful chocolate man with a nice build, a shiny bald head, and amazing skin. With him was a Bible, and I could tell he was worried.

He removed himself from the room, and I was left alone with her. I believe my cousin Toni came in when he stepped out. I always was curious if I should've brought my brothers with me, because maybe, she would have responded to them. So many hypothetical questions circulated my brain during that time. So, she and I were finally completely alone; she was just hooked up to the machines.

I kissed her cheek and said, "Hey, Mommy. I miss you. The boys miss you." Then, I told her, "They say you won't wake up. Let's prove them wrong. Open your eyes; lift your finger. You're not brain dead. You can't be… You just spoke to me on Christmas Day. Mommy, can you hear? The boys need you. I need you!"

After a few quiet moments, I then began to say I thought they were supposed to save her, with tears rolling down my face. I don't remember all that I said, but I remember shouting and screaming and crying hysterically, saying, "Why couldn't you save her? You were supposed to save her. No one did their job!" My cousin came in and grabbed me because they told her they were going to call the police to escort me out. It was my first time seeing her in days, and her body was there, but nothing was working. There was no brain activity. Well, how do you expect an eighteen-year-old to respond to her mom laying lifeless on a hospital bed? My cousin grabbed me, hugged me, and told me that it was going to be okay and that she was sorry. There were large snot bubbles and tears flowing like rivers while I sniffled, shaking my head, saying no, as we proceeded to the elevator.

She took me downstairs to the cafeteria. I believe that at that point, my heart was broken into a million pieces. My heart was lying upstairs in a hospital bed, not completely dead, but in transition. I lost myself in more ways than I realized. I still couldn't fathom it.

The next day, we met with the staff: my father, my grandparents, my aunts and uncles, myself, and the head neurologist who had been on vacation. My family wanted to sue because the hospital tried to save the fetus and not my mother. The medicine they prescribed gave my mother multiple strokes, so her speech was slurred. She lost functionality on her left side, and the mini seizures happened quite frequently. At the time, they told us the seizures were simply muscle spasms.

The lead neurologist said if he had been there, he would've been able to save her. We were in a meeting deciding on the next steps. *What are the next steps? What do we do next? What can we do? How will we survive this? My mother has always been around. This can't be real. How will this impact my life?*

We went home after the meeting. I was still hoping, praying, and fasting for a miracle to transpire. However, my dad came to me and said we had to make a decision because she was connected to the machines. I'm still not sure how I survived it. I reminded him that my mother never wanted to be a vegetable; she always stated that. We knew what we had to do. At this juncture, my family members were all in support of my father's decision because he was her husband. My father consulting me allowed me to understand how important this decision was. We told them to remove the machines. I stepped out. My friends, Ray and Brock, came up the elevator to see me and her.

I gave them the news, and they asked, "How is she?"

I said, "We are pulling the plugs."

They were so shocked as to how calm I was. At that time, I was calmer because two days prior, I had just had a mental breakdown. I was really stoic and in shock. I believe this is when I started to move on autopilot.

What do you say to the little toddlers who are looking for their mom? At this time, everyone was gathering at my grandparents' house—family, friends of the family, high school friends, childhood friends, my father's friends. Food galore, but I couldn't eat. I began to lose weight rapidly; by the end of this, I weighed ninety pounds. Everyone wants to know those four words: "How are you doing?" I said, "Okay," but then I shortly stopped. I said, "I'm doing. I'm lost. I miss my mom. My heart is broken."

I did not want to return to school because my mind wasn't there. During this time, harsh things were said to my father. My grandfather said it should've been him. Then, my dad began to say it should have been me. I'm just like, What in the world? Then, we had to settle the accounts. My brothers and I were the beneficiaries. I was eighteen, so I received my portion right away, but my brothers were only three and four years old, so they would receive theirs later.

Then, we had to work on the funeral arrangements. I went to Aikens Funeral Home, which my mother felt had the best work for this service. I remember looking at caskets. I wanted a white one; the inside stated *Mother* with a flower. She would be buried next to my grandmother, Betty, who is my father's mother. Then, we went to the mall to choose what she would wear. I wanted her in white, with a pop of yellow, because she loved all colors, but she said if she had to choose, she would have to go with yellow. I found a white suit from White House Black Market and a yellow sleeveless turtleneck from Express. My mother's sister wore the exact same thing. My hair had been in a long sew-in; I decided to cut it into a long bob. I also wore cream pants with gold details, a white tank, a yellow cropped sweater blazer, and sunglasses.

My godmother did my mother's hair into a bun; she loved a nice bun. My cousin, Renee, did my mother's makeup... she really did look as though she was sleeping. She looked very peaceful. I know she was in constant pain from the migraines she was having. She needed the lights off; she also stopped doing her hair and only wore an Afro for a while. So, to see her lying there still, yet peaceful, I was glad she wasn't in pain, but I knew

I would miss her dearly. I saw her after the finishing touches. Before the wake, there was a slideshow playing memories of her. I snuck out before too many people witnessed me there. Her funeral felt like she was famous. She died very young, at thirty-five; which is just a year older than I am now while writing this. She had been with my father for nineteen years, since she was in high school, but they were only married for three years. I imagined the headline would read, "A young mother dies at thirty-five, leaving behind her three children and her husband. How unfortunate."

Her life was just beginning, in a sense, and it felt like we were all on a new journey that quickly took a halt. Then, we had to start all over again without the matriarch of my immediate family. It didn't seem fair.

Anyhow, there was only standing room at my mother's service. We took a limo to my grandfather's church; the sirens were blaring loudly. I remember we began to line up to file in— my father, my brothers, and I, and then my grandmother. My grandfather and uncle ordained the service; my uncle also did the obituary. I believe they sang "We're Marching to Zion." I remember my dad touching her hand, then leaning in to kiss her. He picked up my baby brother, and he didn't kiss her; he was afraid. Of course, he was. As a baby, I can only imagine what was going through his brain: the image of his lifeless mother, who laughed and chased them frequently, was sleeping. Then, I picked up my eldest brother, and he kissed her. Then, I touched her hand, I kissed her, and I told her how much I loved her. I remember people singing, such as her friend from work and my longtime friend, Sir Brock; he sang and danced on my behalf. There were flowers galore. I had my head down in my lap, and I can recall everyone tapping me or rubbing my shoulder, saying, "This is your aunt. I love you. I'm sorry, and I'm here if you need me."

After everyone visited her body, they closed the casket. Then, I walked up to her and I just hugged it. Oh, how I wish she could've hugged me back. This was a turning point in my life; it was so surreal. I remember her saying to me one day when she did my hair, back when she had to speak up for me, "I'm not always going to be here. You have to learn how to do this." I'm grateful she made me do certain adult things because she was right—she wasn't always going to be here. Even though that was the truth and the most logical thing for her to tell me, I would always respond, "Why would you say that?", and she would say, "Because it's the truth. If I'm not here, I need you to be able to do this on your own." In the hospital, when she told me to take care of my brothers, I did it wholeheartedly. To some people, she meant it figuratively, but I tried to do everything. I never wanted my brothers to want for anything. After the funeral, which was beautiful, we went to the gravesite, and then the repast. At the site, there were still so many people.

I remember my brother, Khai, saying as she was being lowered into the ground, "She's not coming back."

My heart broke. He was just four.

My grand-aunt replied, "No, baby; she's not."

Then reality hit me that she was gone forever.

Unfortunately, my baby brothers have to grow up without the woman who loved them with her whole life. It was a very sad day, although the sun was shining brightly.

Afterwards, I changed into some casual clothes, went to the repast, and left immediately. I literally stayed for around ten to fifteen minutes… My cousin's boyfriend asked me if I was ready to go, and I said yes. I wore a knitted shirt and jeans. I left and went back to my grandparents' house. I was hurting in a way I never knew I could hurt. I didn't understand what was happening. It felt like an out-of-body experience. *She's officially gone.* I didn't want to stay at home because I could feel her spirit, and it felt strange to be there without her.

Once my family left, I felt out of place… I was out of touch with my dance company, my friends, and my family. Then, we had to move. We lost our home. My father lost his job. I felt helpless. What can I do? I have savings, but not enough. Maybe I can get a place, I thought.

Shortly after, I just knew my dad was going to die. I had

done research on wives dying before husbands, and most died a few months later from heartache. I told my dad, "Hey. It looks like you're giving up. You're throwing in the towel... I already lost one parent; I can't lose you, too. So, will you fight to stay alive? We need you!" At this point, we were living with my grandparents, and my father was living at his eldest sister's house. My brother was starting to pee more frequently in the bed at night; I think it was a nervous thing.

One day, he asked for Mom, and I said, "She's an angel now."

He asked, "Is she in heaven?" I said yes with tears in my eyes, and I told him she loved them very much.

I cried a lot because I just felt so horrible for them. I at least had eighteen years, but they only had three and four years with her. It is so devastating. I never knew my heart could hurt the way it did when my mother died.

My relationship with my father began to change drastically during that time. I thought we would get a home and that he would pick up the pieces to put our family back together, but that did not happen. There became a rift between us, unfortunately... We both were so angry, hurt, and confused. I don't believe he felt he could do it—as in, raise his children without her. He doubted his ability to be my father, and at this point, I felt like I lost both parents.

I began to grieve for my father. I never thought about it that way, but honestly, on December 28th, 2006, I lost both my parents. How do you grieve a physical being whose soul is so detached? The person is still living, but they are not connected to this world. I still kept my faith and tried to keep my father empowered, as well. I kept informing him that he had a purpose-driven life, although I was an "adult" at eighteen, according to this system: "I need you, and my brothers especially need you."

During this time, I didn't feel as though I was ready to navigate this world. *Have I learned enough? What do I do now?* I did not feel as though I was ready to be an adult. *I don't feel* prepared to be the parent, the adult. I'm so confused. I am so lost without her. Mother, where art thou? Did you have to leave? Lord, help me. I could recall myself praying and journaling all the time. No dancing for me, no shopping. I stopped doing all the things that I enjoyed with her and that she loved to see me do. I read The Four Agreements and The Prayer of Jabez during this time. My family wanted me to see a therapist, but I was convinced they believed I was crazy, and rightfully so. I had gone from the bubbly, beautiful young woman to the distant, angry young woman. I felt very isolated during this time. I was very reclusive, and I spoke to God a lot. As faithful as I was, I still became very angry with God.

Why would You take my mom away?

How could You take my mom away from us?

She was only thirty-five. I used to become so terrified about my birthday, praying and hoping and wishing I could make it to another year, and the closer I got to thirty-five, the more frightening it became. I started doing research in my family, and I saw that my great-grandmother expired very young.

My grandmother was six, and her eldest sister reared her; she was eighteen, like me. Then, my great-grandfather moved to another city and left his daughter to raise his children. So, I started to question everything.

Is this a generational curse?

Will I die before I have children?

Will I die young?

My thoughts became a little dark.

Is this my reality?

Was I created to repopulate and never see my creation become an adult?

I know it sounds insane, but sometimes, my thoughts

were dark because I was searching for my light. In this time, I still prayed, I still fasted. I got back in school to get my AA degree. I was traumatized. I experienced the greatest loss.

Was my mother's death a traumatic experience for me?

Yes, it is, and it's one of the greatest losses.

How do you come back from that?

Where do you go from here?

My heart is broken. I do not like the pain that I'm feeling.

How do I silence the heartache?

How do I move forward?

Do I know what moving forward will look like?

Will I remain stagnant, lost in the space of the unknown?

Unfortunately, I cannot stop and process. I have to keep moving. I have two little boys to take care of, who watch me daily.

So, here I am, Lord.

I am in need of prayer. I am in need of healing. I need the Holy Spirit to intervene on my behalf. Lord, You know my heart. I know I've questioned You lately, but I am hurting and I have no one else to go to. I do not know what to do. I am lost.

Is this punishment for a past life of mine or my mother's?

What do I continuously tell my brothers?

How do I protect them? How will I be able to help the ?

How will this affect all of us?

We are all hurting—my grandparents, my aunts, my uncles, my cousins, my grand-aunts, my father, my siblings, and I. So much has changed in a matter of days. I do not want to cry anymore.

During this time, I remember my grandmother telling me we came from strong women: "Your mother was a very strong woman, and you have her strength and my strength inside of you. So, don't cry so much." I know this could've been taken out of context, her telling me not to cry, but she was just seeing her granddaughter in pain and she wanted to help.

Life is very different now. I began to distance myself and not say too much. I went back to my previous boyfriend, and of course, that didn't last long. I was trying to fill a void, but I did not know it at the time. All I knew was that I had an immense amount of pain that I could not describe, and I had no one to talk to about it with. My heart was broken, and I had to be strong for my brothers, so I pushed through. I journaled and read a million self-help and faith books, and my grief began to lessen, but ultimately, it would come back to haunt me.

If you do not deal with the trauma that you experienced, it will continue to fester. My faith was weakened after this, but I never completely lost it. I questioned God, because He is the only being who could give me the answers that I desired. I continued to go to school because so many people convinced me that this is what my mother wanted for me: "Although you're eighteen years old, you still really cannot make your own decisions." School was always fairly easy because I was taught at a very young age how to study and how to break down what I learn. I could read extensively, I was naturally smart, and I had a lot of discipline instilled in me through my parents and the extracurricular activities I was involved in. So, school kept my mind occupied, but I wasn't giving it my all.

When I first went back after my mother's death, I was floating, traveling from house to house with my brothers attached at the hip. I could not get my bearings. I felt all over the place in some instances, then I felt well-put-together in other instances. I learned to be well-prepared and put together despite all of the things that were happening in my life, which can be difficult to understand. This means I went on autopilot, so I became very robotic in some ways, not showing emotion, not taking anything personally. *Just keep swimming like Dora and Nemo, and you* will not drown. But the body continues to keep score, and as we heal, sometimes, we find it difficult to navigate what we feel or the reality of our internal experience. We continue to be set in a trauma, stagnant and not fully alive in the present.

Where do we go from here?

Do you continue to live?

These are questions that I continuously ask myself. I want to heal. I want to feel free. I want to be myself again without the effects of my grief. However, my grief is a part of my journey. It's not all of who I am, but it's a part of my story.

I know so many people want to know where I am now… literally, where am I right now in my healing journey. Before writing this chapter, I was in a better place mentally, physically, spiritually, and emotionally. I thought I had healed certain wounds, but maybe I just took a swab, cleansed them, and covered them with a bandage. When I made the choice to write this chapter, my goal would be to help others deal with their grief and a major loss…This chapter flipped my world upside down. Before this began, I felt fuller, more healed, more stable.

With this chapter, I felt chaos, pure chaos—not relief, not joy. I was frozen in time. I couldn't journal; I couldn't read. My focus began to shift; my relationship was altered. This is fifteen years later. *Why am I feeling like the insecure eighteen-year-old woman whose mother just passed away? I go to therapy; I have been doing the work for fifteen years.* However, I was going to therapy and only touching the surface of this because I did not understand the root from which this seed was planted. I began to feel the hurt and pain all over again. How is this even possible? I knew I would relive some of it, but not at the expense of everything I have built. I have been down this road. What in the world is happening to me?

I tried speaking to my father about it, and he was just baffled… He would always ask, "Why would you even want to write about this?" Honestly, I've been an advocate for healing for fifteen years. It is so easy for me to help and assist others with their healing. However, had I known this would be the outcome, I probably would have said no. Yet, I knew if I was going through this with my grief, there were other people experiencing something similar.

Grief is very difficult and challenging at times. Everyone wants to help, but most do not have a clue how to help you. From this, I created Heal Love. Now, Heal Love started because I got into a horrible accident a year ago and felt like I had to start all over again. However, with this chapter, I also realized I COULD NOT HELP OTHERS HEAL IF I COULD NOT POUR INTO MYSELF FIRST. So, let me tell you about Heal Love. Heal Love is a movement created to empower people who have felt neglected, unseen, and unheard, and whose lives had become difficult while dealing with trauma. Heal Love is a celebration that empowers people who have felt less confident because of the uncertainty of who they are outside of their traumas and healing journeys. So, with this movement, I created affirmations to help reaffirm the beliefs that were once inside of you, to reaffirm the confidence that you lack that took away from your passion, to reignite the burning fire that is inside of you, to reaffirm a love of self, and to reaffirm that all things are possible with God.

I now know that some people become traumatized, and they become stuck... stopped in their growth because they can't integrate new experiences into their lives. Most people who have trauma approach everything in fragments. I know that since my own trauma, I've slowed down. I do not respond hastily. I choose to not be triggered by my past. The movement I've created is helping women become more confident in their bodies, which translates throughout the rest of their lives. Healing is not linear. Healing does not have a quick fix. You cannot just fly to Miami, pay $20,000, and expect a miracle. Every day, you work to become more at peace, more stable, more secure, more in love with your whole being. You will have ebbs and flows, hills and valleys. Healing is constant. However, you do not have to live in your past. It happened, but you can grow through it and move forward. You have to be willing to do the work that is required of you.

Heal Love was a thought that transcended into a class, a journal, and soon, a retreat. Yes, we all have experienced atrocities, but we can not allow those things to take over our lives. We will be present. We will be free. We will love. We will smile again. We will laugh. We will embrace our journeys. We can be the change that we seek. This is not our final destination. This is just a chapter in our book. We have the power to live each day as fully as we possibly can. Nothing or no one can live our lives for us. While we journey, we must stay steadfast in our faith, praying and meditating and fasting. Faith comes by hearing, and hearing comes by the word of the Lord.

Although I questioned God in the beginning, I ultimately felt His presence and knew that he always has His hand on my life. I could not have accomplished any of my goals without Him. He makes all things better. When I fast, pray, and meditate, my mind is clear. Clarity provides room for exploration, discovery, and creativity. I want to integrate and implement everything that I have learned on my healing journey.

I want you to not be the insecure girl who cried in the bathroom stall, trying to understand why she has to live the rest of her life without a mother, a confidant, a best friend, a support system. You are not that girl. But you are brave, brilliant, intelligent, talented, loving, caring, passionate, honest, and free to be all that you desire to be. Be the role model that you seek! Love your flaws. Become so intimate with yourself that no one can tell you whose you are.

Thank you for reading about my grief... Good or bad, I own it, and my prayer for you is that you do the same.

My Prayer for You Today, A Prayer for Good Grief:

Lord,

Create in me an internal peace, safety, and security that I did not have in my past. Let my love for You and myself exude in all that I do. Let me accept the things that I cannot change, like my grief and my past. Allow me to have the courage to change the things that are not of You, and ultimately, let me have the wisdom to understand my purpose and my journey. Let me rest in Your power and meditate day and night. Please continue to keep me strong in faith. Guard my mind and open my heart. Let me not be so quick to judge because everyone has a story, and we are all going through something. Let me become expressive and not hold everything in so I do not explode on the wrong person because I could not communicate my thoughts clearly. Father, You know I desire to be more like You. Allow me to surrender to Your love for me. Grant me peace that surpasses all understanding. Enlarge my territory as You continuously bless me and those whose lives I come into contact with! We know all things are possible to those who believe in Your will!

Amen.

La'Dreauna Johnson

Chapter 4

All Hell Broke Loose

This part of my life is called:

All Hell Broke Loose

It was March 2013. I was sitting in the Popeyes drive-through line when my phone began to ring. As I glanced down at the name of the caller, I was unimpressed, and I answered with hesitation.

"Hey. What's up?" I began.

"Nothing; just checking on you," the caller replied. "What are you doing?"

"I'm in the drive-through, about to order some food."

"Oh, okay. I was thinking you're probably pregnant, and that could explain why you've been so moody and mean."

Taking a moment to look at the phone before responding, I started thinking back to our last encounter. My mind went back to the night we last slept together. The entire night replayed in my head in a matter of seconds.

"Lex," he continued.

"It's no way I'm pregnant," I snapped. "Don't even call me, talking like that. My period isn't due yet. I have another two weeks."

"I'm just saying that you're pregnant, which can explain the attitude."

"I'm not, and I'm about to order my food. I'll talk to you later."

I did just that. I ordered a Shrimp Tackle Box from Popeyes off Wesley Chapel Road in Decatur, Georgia, and drove to work, not thinking twice about that call. I assumed he called with the intentions of fucking up my day, and I had every intention of not letting him.

Fast forward three weeks. My period never showed up. I was, indeed, pregnant. My mind raced as I came to the realization that I had to tell him. To be honest, I also thought of the ramifications of me not telling him and just raising my baby alone and in peace. That thought quickly passed as I realized that I would be denying my child a relationship with his or her father.

As I scrolled through the contact list in my phone, I realized that this conversation could go one of two ways: He would be happy and excited, and I would hang up feeling relieved; or, he would be excited, but I wouldn't feel relieved because now, he would require more out of me and my time. He could be a lot at times—extremely demanding and very outspoken. He could also come off as rude and arrogant. I didn't know which route he would take after finding out the news. Those thoughts started to bring on anxiety and a little nervousness.

I found his name and clicked on his number. The phone started to ring. As the phone rang, all I could think about was him saying to me, "I want a baby. You always have your niece with you, but you got rid of mine. I want us to be here with my baby. You got rid of mine without even consulting me."

To add context to the relationship, we met when I was a junior in college. I believe I was twenty-one, and he was exactly ten years older than me, thirty-one. Although I was attending school at Bethune-Cookman University, I grew up in Tallahassee and always participated in FAMU's homecoming activities. We met at a FAMU homecoming game.

We hit it off immediately. He would always drive to Daytona Beach, Florida to visit me while I was in college. Every time he would come, it was always a good time, filled with nonstop laughter. At the time, I was young and not looking for a serious relationship with him.

As the year passed, I graduated from Bethune-Cookman

University and relocated to Miami. He was actually the one who moved all of my stuff from Daytona to Miami. During this move, his crazy side started to show. I remember driving when he snatched my phone out of my hand and went through it. He found some old text messages and became so upset that he jerked the wheel, almost causing an accident, and then threatened to leave me at the gas station. The rest of the trip was a nightmare. God allowed us to make it to my new condo in Miami safely, but he was still upset, and it showed. He became careless with how he handled my furniture, breaking the glass table and the mirror to my dresser.

From that point on, the relationship would never be the same. During the three years I lived in Miami, he would pop up randomly to visit me. Each trip, I noticed I began to not enjoy his company as much. On one of those trips, I became pregnant. Knowing the type of man he showed me he could be towards me, I decided to abort the baby. At that time, I felt like this was the best decision for me. I recently graduated, it was the middle of the recession, and I was working at Coach in the Dolphin Mall making minimum wage. Not only did I not want to procreate with him, but I also could not afford to have a baby. So, I did what I felt was best for me.

Of course, I told him the situation. I let him know that I was not ready for a baby and that I had moved forward with my decision to abort the baby, thinking that he would be reasonable and have some type of understanding. He was the opposite. He lost his mind, and for the next two to three years, he would bring up the baby every opportunity he had and use it as a low blow in arguments. He would constantly tell me, "You got rid of my baby," "You're the one who got an abortion without my consent," or, "You made the decision to have an abortion without even considering how I felt." All that did was make me hate myself for telling him about the baby. I was filled with so much regret, not only because I had the abortion, but also because I shared something so personal with him. It felt like I had a spot on my clean reputation, and because he had no other way of hurting me, he used that one decision I made against me for years.

Now, here I was, in a similar situation with him again. I was nervous about sharing this news with him. But this was the guy who had actually *begged* me for another baby; this was the guy who acted so hurt by my decision to terminate the previous pregnancy. So, here I was, years later, pregnant by the same guy who had already shown me his true colors. Not only was I disappointed in myself; I was also angry with myself. I allowed myself to end up here, in this same spot with him again. Thinking back to the night we conceived, I distinctly remember not wanting to be intimate with him. I told him that I was not having sex with him.

He replied by saying, "You got me fucked up," and proceeded to get on top of me.

Seeing that there was no way out of this situation and he had every intention on having sex with me, I then made another request: "Can you please put a condom on?"

He replied, "You got me fucked up."

Now, he was having sex with me without a condom.

I made one final request: "Can you please pull out? I do not want to get pregnant."

He replied, "You got me fucked up."

As he finished, he ejaculated inside of me, ignoring all my requests. I jumped up immediately to use the restroom, trying to push it out. As I sat on the toilet, I could see him laying down in my bed. All I could do was yell at him, telling him how fucked up his actions were and that I could not handle another abortion. I remember saying, "If I'm pregnant, I'm keeping this baby."

At the time, I was more upset about him ejaculating in me more than the entire encounter itself. At the time, I did not know this was a form of rape. In fact, it was years later, as I was having lunch with my current boyfriend, when I realized it. We started talking about women trapping men with babies, and how men can trap women, as well. I explained to him that no woman wants to be a single mom, and that men will intentionally get women pregnant to have ties with them for the rest of their lives. I explained the story of the night I got pregnant, and as I was at the table fighting back tears, he looked at me in the eyes and said, "Baby, that sounds like rape. That is some crazy shit." I left lunch and drove home crying because, it indeed, was rape. I was clear with each request, and each one of them went ignored. I called my mom and my sisters crying. I had told everyone the story in past; no one told me that I was raped. Regardless of us having an intimate history, on that night and in that moment, I said, "NO."

The phone rang again.

"What's up, Lex?"

"Nothing too much," I replied. "Are you in Atlanta?"

"No," he said. "Why? What do you have going on?"

"When will you be here?" I asked.

I don't know when I'll be back that way. Why what do you need?"

"Just call me when you get here," I requested.

"If it's something we need to talk about, tell me now, because I won't be there no time soon."

"Just call me when you get here. I have to go," I said, regretting the call.

"Now, you got me wanting to know. So, tell me what's up," he implored.

As he started to go off on a tangent about him wanting to know right then and demanding that I tell him, I just blurted out the two words: "I'm pregnant."

He was extremely quiet. We were both just quietly holding the phone, waiting to see who was going to say something to end the silence. I made up my mind that I would wait for him to say something. I wanted his reaction. I knew that his next words would set the tone for this entire pregnancy.

He finally spoke.

"Damn, Lex."

"What do you mean?"

"Damn, Lex. You done got pregnant."

I was completely quiet, not knowing where he was going with that comment, not knowing if it was a joke. His next line immediately let me know that it was no joke. He was dead ass serious.

He said to me, "Whose baby is it? It can't be mine."

I immediately rebutted, "Are you serious right now?"

He went on to tell me that he was not ready for kids, and demanded that I have another abortion. He knew how much regret I had from the first abortion; he also knew that I vowed to never do that again. He knew everything that we had gone through, yet he still could fix his mouth to say those words to me. I was stunned by his reaction. This was the same guy who would constantly tell me how my decision to have an abortion hurt him and how much he wanted a baby. Was this that same guy, or was this someone new? From that day forward, the guy I knew for years switched up on me and became someone else, someone totally different.

We got into a huge argument, and I hung up in tears. I was filled with every emotion: sadness, fear, and confusion. On that day, I knew I was in this situation by myself. I knew that he was not the type of man I wanted to spend the next eighteen years of my life co-parenting with. Over the next few weeks, he became extremely disrespectful, calling me only to yell and belittle me. He called me every name in the book except for a child of God. He would scream things like, "Bitch, that's not my baby! You need to have an abortion like you did last time!" I mean, he was *awful* to me. He was so hurtful and so disrespectful that I had to block his number. When he was having a bad day, he would call using a private number just to curse me out and try to make me have a bad day, too. In order for me to protect my emotions and my mental health, I had to completely detach myself from him. I had to tell myself that the old guy who I used to love was gone; he was truly someone else now.

To get away from the situation completely, I decided to move back to Tampa. I left the job I was working at because he used to pop up there. I moved out of my townhouse and moved in with my aunt. He could no longer just pop up to my house or my job, and he could not get in contact with me because he was blocked. I thought that the move would bring me some peace of mind, but it didn't. I was so hurt by the turn of events that I was borderline depressed. I blamed myself for everything. *How was I so stupid? How did I let this happen again? How did I let this man trick me for so many years?*

This part of my life is called:

Living Faith by Faith

I know you're wondering, *Well, where does her faith kick in?* The honest answer is that through it all, I always exercised my faith. I've always had a strong connection with God. I grew up in the church—in fact, my grandfather is a pastor, and he still has his church in Tampa. I would spend my summers in Tampa, going to NYSP Summer Camp in the day, and at night, we would always end up at church. Between the different revivals, Bible study nights, feeding the community, or just cleaning the church, we were always there. I remember telling my grandad that I was tired of spending my summer in church, and he said, "This is the best place to be if you want to keep the devil out of you." I said all of that to say, I knew right from wrong. I knew what God approved of and what God despised. I know how Christians felt about abortions. It was knowing that I went against everything I believed in that made me regret my decision.

As I mentioned, I graduated in 2009 at the peak of the recession. Not only did I move to Miami in the middle of the recession—I moved to downtown Miami. Thank God I was able to work and save while I was in college, because finding a decent paying job was impossible. I remember calling my mom and dad daily, and I would be fighting back tears because I did not know how my future would look. I did not know how long I would be working a job making $7.25 an hour with a bachelor's degree. I was disappointed because I did everything right. Everyone said, "Make good grades in high school so you can get scholarships for college." I did just that. I made good grades and had a tutor at Sullivan, who helped me make a high score on the ACT. I was awarded the Florida Bright Futures Scholarship, which, at the time, would have paid for 75 percent of my tuition if I attended any public four-year college or university in the state of Florida. Of course, I decided to go to a private HBCU. Go figure. While in college, I was told, "Make good grades, and you'll have better opportunities." Well, I made decent grades for four years straight, even taking classes at TCC or FSU every summer, just to graduate in a recession.

Nothing was going as I planned, but God had His own plans for my life. Although I was working part-time in the mall, I still had so much free time on my hands. I was used to always having a full schedule; even as a child, my mom kept me busy, I was in dance; I was a cheerleader; I was a part of the Delta Teen Challenge program; I was a part of the Youth Ministries at church. In college, I was a full-time student, and I worked part-time for three out of the four years. From as early as I can remember, I was always busy; I always had a schedule; I always had somewhere to be. Well, now, here I was, a twenty-one- or twenty-two-year-old with nothing but free time. No set schedule and nowhere to be. I did not know how to cope with the drastic chain of events. I had never even heard of a recession until 2008. I did not know how to plan or properly prepare for it.

Most people struggle through college financially, making do with the little they have because of the bigger reward that was promised to them once they graduate. We are all told, "You will get a good paying job once you obtain your degree"—the high-paying job, living financially free, the 401k all were the rewards we were working so hard to receive. So, imagine our shock when it was finally our turn to be adults and make adult money, everything was on a freeze, and no one was hiring. Corporations were laying off floors of people in one day. So, the people with years of real work experience got the better paying jobs; some of them even ended up with part-time mall jobs, like me. Everything we were promised was no longer available to us. Everything was a lie. The value of a degree was no longer there. We could not separate ourselves from the crowd. We were all in this economic shitshow together.

It was during that time in my life when I had all the time in the world. I started giving that time to God. When I was living in Miami, I started to attend New Birth Baptist Church off of 135th Street. I did not join the church, but I began to spend a lot of time there. I would attend services on Sundays and mid-week services on Wednesdays. If there were any community events, I would attend those, too. At the time, I did not have cable, and the only reason I had internet is because my Pops put me on his account. Every night, I would read the Bible before going to sleep. I would study it. I found myself in church a few times out of the week. All those summers I had spent at my granddad's church somehow prepared me for this moment. I somehow gravitated towards church because it was a safe place for me; it was familiar. Church gave me hope and faith; it also gave me a schedule. I had places to be again; I had things to do again. I was meeting people left and right. In church was right where I needed to be.

I can recall sitting in New Birth one Wednesday night and looking up at all the scrolls that were hanging. Each scroll had a different Jehovah listed, and they all explained the different ways God shows up and the names He is called. I was so drawn to the one that said "Jehovah—Jireh: The Lord will provide." I loved this message so much that I made those words the screen on my phone. I was at a time in my life where I could not provide for myself. I was running through my savings because although we were in a recession, the bills did not stop. Although no one was making decent money and companies were laying people off left and right, the bills did not stop. The world did not stop. We had to try our best to keep up and continue as normal. It was during that time that I knew Jehovah Jireh, because the Lord was my provider. God was making a way out of no way for me. I had no money, but I began to meet people who would look out for me. Random family members would send me money; the lady at the Publix by my condo would give me discounts on my groceries, and every week, my Dad would send me money. I remember pulling up to the gas station to put five dollars in my tank, and some man offered to fill my tank for me. I mean, God was sending people to me out of the woodworks. Even my ex-boyfriend's mother took me grocery shopping once. She did not limit me; she allowed me to stock up.

All of my needs were met day after day, week after week. God provided and placed so many people in my path who wanted to bless me. It was also at New Birth that I learned what is now my favorite Bible verse, Jeremiah 29:11: "'For I know the plans I have for you,' declares the Lord. 'Plans to prosper you and not harm you, plans to give you hope and a future.'"

That verse alone is enough to make a nonbeliever want to become a believer. The verse alone is enough to put any negative thoughts you have about your current situation or your future to rest. That verse alone should soothe your soul. God tells us everything we need to know about our future. Jeremiah 29:11 told me a few things:

- Only God knows our future, so stop overthinking it.

- In our future, God is going to prosper us, so stop letting the enemy see you sweat. In other words, stop worrying about the weapons that form against you because God said He is going to prosper you.

- God does not have plans to harm us, so if it is happening to you, it is also happening for you. "All things work together for the good of those who love Him."

- God has a future for us that is filled with hope, so always remember that your future is hopeful. Keep the faith and trust that God has a rewarding future planned for you.

I used to meditate on this verse daily, often with tears in my eyes, but faith in my heart. I am a firm believer that God is a promise keeper, and Jeremiah 29:11 is filled with promises for our future. I want to encourage you to carry this verse in your heart with you daily and remember that you have a bright future ahead of you. No matter how bleak your current situation may seem, no matter how hard life is for you today, God is going to prosper you. God is going to bring you through it. You will be victorious. Don't lose your faith.

It was those early years of being in church and building my relationship with God that have helped me get through some of my worst days. Although I did not have the most ideal pregnancy, I would thank God daily for my daughter. I exercised my faith by continuing to show gratitude and constantly praying for my daughter. I was told that your baby can feel all of your emotions, so instead of allowing myself to be sad and depressed, I would intentionally find joy in small things daily. I had to condition my mind to only focus on the positives of my pregnancy. I was a healthy, educated twenty-six-year-old woman, carrying a healthy and beautiful baby girl. I would tell myself that I was blessed to be able to conceive because there are millions of women who are not as fortunate. I had to recognize the many ways in which God was blessing me. I could have easily focused on the negative. I could have lost my faith and told myself that I was a statistic, that I was adding to the number of fatherless kids, that I would now only be seen as a single mom, that no one would want to marry me because I came with too much baggage." The list of negative thoughts could go on and on, but I would not allow myself to focus on those things. Instead, I journaled. I wrote notes and emails to my daughter. I spoke life into her. I told her that she was the best thing that ever happened to me. I told her that God himself picked her for me, and me for her.

On the day she was born, I had my family in the room with me. She was surrounded by love when she entered this world. From that day forward, all she has ever known is love. Her father, on the other hand, is in and out of her life. He did not come to the hospital for her birth because it was Classic Weekend, a weekend during which FAMU and Bethune-Cookman go head-to-head in a football game. Apparently, the game was more important. However, he did come a few days later to see her and take pictures of her. After that, she did not see him again until a few months later, when I moved back to my parents' house in Tallahassee.

During that visit, she screamed the entire time he held her. He continued to be disrespectful to me, blaming me for her not having a connection with him. Throughout the two years I was living with my parents, he might have stopped by five times. Often, it would end in an argument because, in his exact words, I forced him to be a father to a baby that he did not want. He told me to have an abortion and I didn't listen. Every visit was an up-and-down roller-coaster of emotions. After a while, the words were no longer hurtful; him not showing up as an active parent didn't bother me. I had to grow thick skin if I wanted him to have some type of relationship with his daughter. No matter how messed up the relationship was, I still wanted my daughter to know that she had a dad, even though he was horrible.

I recall going on a family outing to the mall with my mom, my sister, my niece, and my daughter. We arrived at the Governor's Square Mall as it opened. I put my daughter in her stroller, and as we were walking through the mall, I saw her dad. We locked eyes, he looked down at her in the stroller, and he walked right past her as if she did not exist. As he walked past us, I noticed a young woman walking a few steps behind him. Then it dawned on me: He couldn't acknowledge his daughter or me because this new girl didn't know about us. As I watched them walk off, all I could do was shake my head in complete disgust. What kind of man—what kind of dad—was he, that he could walk past his baby without any form of acknowledgement? I guess the same kind who preferred to see a game over the birth of his daughter.

I tried not to hate him and to exercise forgiveness, but he made it extremely hard. My battle with forgiveness became even more complicated. I struggled with the fact that he begged me to have his baby one day, then cursed me a month later for actually becoming pregnant. I struggled with the fact that he intentionally got me pregnant just to make me a single mom. I struggled with the fact that he told me he would not help me with her financially because that would be making it easy on me and that he wanted me to struggle. I struggled with the fact that I asked for fifty dollars a week to help with Pampers, and he said no; I was living with my parents and had no bills, so I should be able to find enough money for Pampers. I struggled with the fact that when I filed for child support, the calls and disrespect got worse. To end all the extra drama, I withdrew my child support application and asked God to provide for me like He had so many times before.

I called on Jehovah Jireh to make a way for me and my daughter. I asked my daughter's father to walk away from us; I asked him to let me raise her alone, in peace. I reminded him that legally, he had no rights because he was not there for the birth. His name was not on the birth certificate, and because he denied her throughout the entire pregnancy, I gave her my last name. I begged him to let us live in peace. I told him that no one knew that she's his daughter and that I would not tell anyone if he could just let me raise her drama-free and in peace. Of course, he would not agree to it. He was set on making my life miserable. Eight years later, I can count on two hands how many times he's physically seen her. The random one-hundred-dollar gifts he's given her in eight years equal less than eight hundred dollars.

She is extremely bright; she's always happy and very outgoing. She has a heart of gold, always willing to put her wants on the back burner to make others happy. She has never missed out on any extracurricular activities, her clothes and shoes are always clean, and she's always had a roof over her head. Since having her, my life has changed drastically. I made a vow to myself and to her that we would never ask her dad for money again. She gave me motivation that I did not have before her. I became so driven to never be broke again. I became the woman, the mom, who she would one day be proud of. I did not get here on my own. It was God and God alone who was meticulous with every step of my life.

This part of my life is called:

Double for My Trouble

For you to fully see God's hand in my life, I have to go back a little. It was 2014. My daughter was eight months old, and I had moved back into my childhood home to live with my parents. I went from being on my own, having a condo in downtown Miami from 2009 to 2011, and having a townhouse in Decatur for 2011 to 2013 to sharing my childhood bedroom with my infant daughter. In between those years, I lived in Tampa with my aunt for a few months of my pregnancy. I felt as if I was moving backwards. Although I recognized that moving back home was the best option available to me at the time, I still felt like a failure.

I made the decision to move back home because once I had my daughter, from the time she came out until she was about five years old, she cried for me, kicking and screaming. She was not the easy baby that they show in movies, taking long naps and enjoying car rides. In fact, I stopped driving with her for a year because the one and only time I drove with her as an infant in the car seat, she cried so much that she threw up. It sounded like she was choking on it, so I turned around for a quick second to look at her, and I hit the car in front of me. Thank God it wasn't a hard hit, and there was no damage, but I learned my lesson, and I would not drive with her in the car with me for her entire first year.

I made the decision to breastfeed her due to all the health benefits, and it was much cheaper than buying formula. I had no clue that breastfeeding would create such a bond between us that she would literally scream if she could not see me. If I walked into another room, she would scream until I was back in her sight. I remember taking showers and putting her in her bouncer in the restroom just so she could see me. I remember crying in the shower because I felt like I never would have a minute alone or to myself. Around this time, my sister, Toni, moved back home, too. She, too, was a single mom, and she had my niece. My niece was a cool baby. She did not cry a lot, and because she was two years old at the time, she was obsessed with her little cousin.

One day, my mom came to us, told us that a position was available at her job, and suggested that one of us apply. Well, of course, I didn't apply. My sister got the position, and because I was now babysitting my niece every day, she paid me. I finally was making some type of money, and I was able to afford my daughter's necessities without a problem. My older sister,

Vandora, was also pregnant and due any day. She was in the Dental Hygienist program at Tallahassee Community College. In this program, each student could only miss a certain number of days before they would be forced to start the program all over. Well, she had my nephew by cesarean and had to return to school three weeks later. Naturally, she asked me to keep him for her because I was already staying home with my daughter and niece. I had officially become "Auntie Daycare."

My days started extremely early. My nephew would get dropped off no later than 7:00 a.m. every day, and my mom, sister, and Pops all headed to work around 8:00 a.m. Oftentimes, the first person would return home after 6:00 p.m. To this day, that was one of the hardest jobs I ever had. I had to get everyone on the same schedule, and because they were all very different ages, I had to try to teach my niece numbers, letters, and songs, and find educational movies for her to watch in between nursing my daughter and feeding my newly born nephew. My niece was very smart, and she caught on to everything quickly. She became my saving grace. She would sing to them and bounce them in their bouncer whenever I needed to cook or make bottles. She was somehow able to keep them quiet long enough for me to get a few things done.

My mom recognized just how sad I had become and started taking a few days off here and there to give me a break. I found a personal trainer, and I started seeing him three to four times a week. I also volunteered to do all the grocery shopping. I recognized that I needed some time for myself, so I filled my free time with working out and a lot of shopping at Publix. Oftentimes, when I'm out and I see women struggling with a crying infant, I always compliment them and tell them that they are doing a great job because I know how hard motherhood can be, especially if you stay at home with the kids everyday. It can take a toll on you mentally. I felt as if I no longer knew how to hold an conversation with adults without sounding dumb. My conversations were filled with ABCs and 123s.

Another way I spent my time was in church on Sunday mornings. Once Sunday, the dean of the School of Journalism at

FAMU was the guest speaker at Sunday school. I remember my sister, Toni, bumping me with her elbow and saying, "You should go talk to her. She's a woman taking care of business." She convinced me to share my story with her. I stepped out on faith and listened to my big sister, Toni. The dean was so moved by my story that she created a Media Sales Position for me to work under her at the School of Journalism. God was moving in my life, and this was just the beginning.

Once I started my new position, I had an instant connection with the dean's assistant, Genevieve. Genevieve was my saving grace. Remember how long it had been since I had adult conversations or even sent business emails? She had to help me get polished. She taught me how to speak and sound educated when in a room full of doctors and professors. I would send her my emails first to review before I sent them to the faculty and staff of the department. She helped ease me back into work life. At the time, she was also a single mom. With her daughter only being a year older than my daughter, we hung out a lot. She was also a member at Bethel AME, which is the church I grew up in and the church my parents were still members of. We spoke a lot about God, and we just kept each other encouraged.

While working at FAMU, students began to migrate to my office, asking for advice and just needing a listening ear. In every situation, I would pray and ask God to put the words that He wanted me to say to each student on my heart. I would ask God to use me to be a vessel to the young men and women who came to me for advice. I had quotes about God and the power of prayer in my office, so whenever anyone walked in, it was clear that I believed in God. During my time at the School of Journalism and Graphic Communication, many young women came to me for relationship advice. There were a few occasions when some of them were pregnant and contemplating abortions. In those moments, I realized how I could truly give advice from the heart and from experience. I would listen to them, and then, I would tell them about my situation and give them the reasons why I made my decision. I would ask them the benefits of having the abortion and the benefits of keeping the baby. Although I had previously

76

gotten an abortion, I would not say I was pro-abortion. I am pro-choice; there is a difference. I do not promote abortion at all; however, I believe that every woman should have a choice in having a baby or terminating the pregnancy.

When these young women would ask me questions about being a single mom, I was honest. I let them know that it is hard, but very rewarding. When they would ask me about having an abortion, I also would let them know that it was hard for me to cope with my decision after the fact. Since I have been in both situations, I can truly say that both decisions had a huge impact on my life. Being able to help those young women helped me forgive myself for having my abortion. If I had not gone through it myself, I would have not been a trusted source for these young women to talk to.

Once, Genevieve and I were planning to participate in the Daniel Fast for Lent. One young woman overheard us talking and asked me for more details. I was able to explain Lent and why we fast during that period, and she decided to participate with us. She explained to me that she was drifting further away from God and wanted to give God another try. She would frequent my office from time to time, giving me updates on her walk with God. Her relationship with God began to blossom. She eventually started going to church more often, and she even was a part of the choir and collegiate ministries. She stopped by my office before her graduation to thank me for taking the time to share my stories about God with her and motivating her to give God another chance. Stories like that one make my heart smile. I was able to help so many find God just from my stories and heartfelt conversations. God was using me, and I loved every minute of it.

One day, as Genevieve and I were completing our TurboTax filing, we started talking about working at FAMU and how much we could both benefit from attending FAMU to pursue a degree. She was planning to apply for her undergrad degree and somehow convinced me to submit an application to the MBA program. I had been avoiding going back to school for years. If you can recall, my first degree had not served me much use. I never actually used it, and nothing drastic happened to my life once I graduated in 2009. Yet, here I was, still living paycheck to paycheck. I enrolled my daughter into a private school that accepted three-year-olds. Although my daughter was, in my opinion, at the best school in Tallahassee, I could barely afford it. There were months when I would have to set up payment arrangements and overdraft my account just to make sure her education was paid for. So, with hesitation, I agreed to apply to the MBA program at FAMU's School of Business and Industry (SBI).

Genevieve had also convinced me to walk over and speak to the Dean of SBI, Dr. Shawnta Friday-Stroud. I did exactly what she suggested and watched how God connected the pieces. Dr. Friday accepted a meeting with me, and after hearing my story, she told me that she would be able to help me obtain funding for my classes. The fellowship program that the dean assigned me to was a program that was under Dr. Jennifer Collins, who just so happens to be in the same sorority and chapter as my mom and sister. It was like every piece was falling into place. God also put it in my spirit to convince my sister, Toni, to apply to the MBA program. I remember telling Toni that two brains are better than one and that it would be so cool for two sisters to graduate from the same program together. I also told her how God was opening doors for me and placing people in place to show me favor. She decided to submit her application to the MBA program, as well. She got in. She was also able to join the same fellowship program that her sorority sister was over.

During that time, I was still working on campus; however, I transitioned from SJGC and was now working in the Sustainability Institute. I must say that it was one of my least favorite jobs. Some days, I would arrive at work at 8:00 a.m., go straight to class after work, and then head straight to the library. Some nights, I would literally leave campus at 2:00 a.m., rush home, get a few hours of sleep, wake up, and do it all over again. Thank God for my village, because between my mother, father, and stepdad, my daughter was able to get picked up from school, helped with homework, fed, and put to bed on time. Although my schedule was all over the place, it was extremely important to me that she would not be affected. After my first two semesters in my MBA program,

I decided to quit that job and focus on graduating. If you have been a part of any graduate programs, you know how critical it is to make all As and Bs. If you make one C, you will have to repeat that class all over. We had a lot of late nights in the library and in SBI, just trying to stay on top of the massive workload.

All of my hard work paid off because I was invited to be a part of the Honor Society. This will always be a huge accomplishment to me because as a child, I struggled for years with reading and speaking. I even had a speech pathologist in elementary school to help me with my word pronunciation. My educational journey was definitely different; in high school, I would be in Honors and Advanced Placement classes, but I would also have to take an Intensive Reading class. In undergrad, I was an average student. I didn't necessarily struggle with school; I graduated with a 3.14 GPA. I was never on the Dean's List, and I never received any of the Cum Laude cords. Receiving this invitation after being out of school over seven years and as a single mom meant the world to me. To top it off, both my parents and my daughter attended my award ceremony. It was a perfect day; all my late nights and hard work had paid off. All of the doubt I had for myself was gone. At that moment, I finally felt good about my education level.

Graduation was near, and I had no plans nor a job lined up, but this time, things felt different. I started to fast, pray more, and really let God lead me. One day, we received an email saying that one of the top retail companies would be on campus to recruit. I convinced some of my other classmates to attend the event with me. Many of us applied to the company, but only a few of us passed the assessment and got an invite to interview. I was one of the few who received the invitation to interview. The company was having an HBCU-themed interview weekend that would take place in Atlanta, Georgia a couple of months out. As I waited for the interview, I also began the process to pursue another one of my longtime dreams of becoming a member of Delta Sigma Theta Sorority, Incorporated.

It was spring of 2018, and everyone was calling and texting me to make sure I saw the flier that the Tallahassee Alumni Chapter of Delta Sigma Theta had posted on their website. I instantly became nervous and excited all at once. Becoming a member of DST was one of the only goals I'd wanted since I was a child. My mother was a member; she pledged when she was an undergrad student at Bethune-Cookman College. This is the only sorority I've ever wanted to join. When I attended BCU, I tried to follow in my mom's footsteps, but I was denied my junior year, and by the time I became a senior, the chapter was suspended. I had been waiting years for the opportunity to apply again, and this was the perfect timing. I had recently graduated with my master's degree, and I had a much higher GPA. It seemed like everything was happening right on time for me. As I waited to hear back from the Deltas, I received my date to interview with the company I had recently applied for. I researched the company and studied their interviewing methods until I was confident in myself. I traveled to Atlanta for the interview; all the while, I was still praying and fasting that I would actually get the job. I did well on all three rounds of interviews, and I was hopeful as I headed back home to Tallahassee.

An hour after my flight landed, I received a call from a member of DST, and she extended me an invitation to interview. I was on cloud nine. I did my research on the sorority and studied their rich history. While on this journey, I was also fasting and in constant prayer. I made it through the interviews by the grace of God because I was literally shaking in my seat the entire time. For some reason, these interviews meant more to me than the ones for the Fortune 500 company that was going to be starting me off at $80,000. Being a Delta was a lifelong dream of mine. The opportunity to join this organization did not come often. Now that I had completed all my interviews, I was in God's waiting room. I was waiting to hear back from someone. Eventually, I got the call from the Deltas. I was selected to join their sorority. As I was on line, I received the call from the company. I was offered a management position in Operations. God had answered my prayers. I was able to fulfill a lifelong dream by becoming a member of Delta Sigma Theta, and I was able to provide my daughter with a better life with my new job. I had never made that kind of money before. I was given a nice sign-on bonus and stocks. Our lives were about to change.

I was assigned a location in Tampa, Florida. My new job was literally located five minutes away from my aunt's house. This was my mom's baby sister, who was a single mom and separated from her children's father at the time. She allowed me and my daughter to move into her beautiful home for my first year. What are the chances that my new job would be located in the city I'm from and walking distance from one of my favorite aunt's houses? God is very meticulous. He had every detail for my life planned; all He wanted me to do was surrender to Him and follow His lead. Things were not perfect at my job; in fact, I ended up hating it. I could not just leave, because along with accepting the sign-on bonus and stocks, I had agreed to stay with them for a minimum of two years.

During this time, I was working four days of twelve-hour shifts on my feet. I would get home, and my feet would be black and blue. Not only was it a lot on my body; I was also mentally drained. I was the only Black female manager in my department. I was so unhappy with my job that I would cry heading in to work.

One day, I called my mom, and as she prayed for me, she mentioned that she would request prayer for me on the prayer line. It went from her requesting prayer for me to her calling me every morning and joining me in on the prayer line. It went from us being a part of one prayer line to two. Every morning, like clockwork, we would stand in prayer together. My mom taking the time to incorporate me on those prayer lines is what kept me sane. The job was only getting worse. I distinctly remember being in a meeting and my very white male manager saying to the entire management team, "If you guys make goal today, Lexie and I will whip and Nae Nae." I was livid again. I was the only Black person in a room of my white counterparts, and was told to do a damn dance if we hit our target. I had to find a way out of that building.

I applied for a transfer to the "Blackest" city I know: Atlanta, Georgia! They gave me a hard time and tried to block me from leaving; however, God had it all worked out. The saying is true, "No man can stop what God has for you." Trust me—they pulled out all the stops to get me to stay and revoke my transfer, but nothing worked. I moved to Atlanta in July of 2019, and with the help of Ashley (who is also an author in this book), I was able to purchase my first home on August 26, 2019. I thought everything was looking up for me.

Well, as it turns out, the culture of the company is embedded in the company. Although I did not have to deal with the long hours or racist remarks, I did have to deal with a new boss who hated me from the day he met me. The level of hate this man had for me was unimaginable. Till this day, no one knows why he did not like me, but everyone knew it, and he made it clear. Thank God I never stopped joining in on those early morning prayer line calls, because I was fighting Goliath on my job daily. Looking back, I know that God was putting all the pieces in place; however, at the time, I could not see it. When you are in the midst of a storm, it's easy to focus on the storm, but you have to put your focus on God. After filing an HR complaint on my manager and working in a hostile environment for a year, it was time for me to move on.

After completing my two years with the company, I applied to become an owner of my own logistics company and to be in partnership with that company. Knowing how much was being said about me by my direct manager and knowing how much influence he had in the company, I applied without letting any of the higher-ups know. In fact, the entire management team applied, and four out of the five of us got it. I put in my two weeks' notice and started my own logistics company. Two years later, I am currently still in partnership with my old company. In hindsight, I know that God made me uncomfortable so that I could get to this space. At the station in Tampa, I was able to establish myself in the company. At the station in Atlanta, I was able to work directly with other owners and see how they structured their companies and pick their brains. It was not until I transferred that I even learned that I could become a partner with the company. It was in Atlanta that the owners would randomly tell me to apply. It was at the station in Atlanta that my counterparts and I all agreed to apply to become partners. It was there that I made the connections that helped me prepare for this. It was managing 168 drivers in

Atlanta that prepared me to manage my fifty drivers.

This all goes back to Jeremiah 29:11—God had a plan for my future. I went from moving back home with my parents to having two houses on two different coasts. I went from not having enough money to pay for my daughter's education to having a savings account for her education. I went from crying on my way to work to laughing with my management team in my office. I went from needing handouts to giving handouts. I went from not having enough to living in the overflow. I went from having a baby with a man that was never there for me to having another baby girl and creating a family with a man who is responsible for and respectful to his family. He is a standup guy and someone that has my back… The partner that I prayed for.

No one can ever tell me that God is not real. God showed up in my life and has kept me to this day. God has restored everything the enemy took from me.

There is a gospel song by Hezekiah Walker, titled "Faithful is our God," that says:

I'm reaping the harvest God promised me

Take back what the devil stole from me

And I rejoice today, for I shall recover it all

Yes, I rejoice today, for I shall recover it all

This is how God works. You will receive double for your trouble. You will recover it all.

Lexie Mutcherson

Chapter 5

The Beauty in Ugly Truth

It was my twenty-fifth birthday, and my boyfriend, Gerald, set up the day for me to follow the directions of these scavenger hunt cards he made. One of the cards said for me to have lunch with a friend. The purpose of the lunch was for me to converse with my friend and to reflect on my new year, which is a practice I've since adopted. The card suggested I discuss with my friend what I had accomplished, what I didn't accomplish, and what my goals for the upcoming year were. During our chat, I mentioned that I would attend cosmetology school one day.

My friend, Gloria, inquired, "Why don't you just do it now?"

After our conversation, I enrolled in cosmetology school within a week and started school about three months later. At the time, I was working a full-time job that I once loved; however, the love began to fade, and I wanted a change of scenery. I graduated college, and although I worked full-time, being at my alma mater, Florida A&M University, made me feel like I had gone nowhere. I was in a rut and wanted to do something I was passionate about. Around age five, I taught myself to braid on a doll, mimicking what I saw my mom doing. To better my skills as a self-taught braider and to get myself out of that rut, I started working at a braiding salon while still employed at FAMU.

What moved me to get behind the chair as a braider in that natural hair salon was my passion for helping women feel confident. I experienced telling friends I wanted to stop relaxing my hair, just for my statement to be followed up with ridicule and disdain for natural hair, so it took a lot of courage for me to stop relaxing my hair. The media and the world around me were not in favor of kinks. Regardless of what was deemed acceptable by society or friends, I followed my own heart and mind, and stopped relaxing my hair. As a braider in a natural hair salon, I planned to empower women with proper education for caring for their hair, filling them with encouraging words and reassurance that they could wear their natural hair and still be beautiful. I remember feeling so rewarded and honored when women came to me for their big chops. I still remember one girl bawling after I cut off her relaxer. She cried healing tears, and she glowed from that moment onward. Over time, it became very clear to me that the braiding salon was not a place where I could grow, and it would be my first experience with a mentor who wanted to see me shine—as long as I didn't outshine her. I wanted to learn more skills outside of braiding and to be in an environment where my growth would be celebrated, so enrolling in cosmetology school made a lot of sense for me, although my mentor at the time was not supportive of my decision.

One of the first lessons that stood out to me as a cosmetology student is when one of my educators stated, "It's not about you." I received her statement as a way of saying it's a cosmetologist's job to serve. I understand now that it's deeper than just serving clients. Although this is my story, it's not about me. It's really about the divine purpose for my life, and I hope my story serves as an example of there being purpose in our pain because the pain is there for a reason.

"Your greatest ministry comes not out of your strengths or talents, but out of your painful experiences."
— Rick Warren (Purpose Driven Life)

I loved cosmetology school, despite the challenging school days of learning at a fast pace and those awkward, racially charged moments from being in a predominantly white space. I looked forward to class and learning new beauty techniques. Although it was fun and very different from a traditional classroom setting, cosmetology school was not easy, and it was tougher than college. My already challenging school days worsened because of a burden I was carrying.

Monday through Wednesday, I worked twenty-four hours weekly at a part-time job, and I would leave work and braid hair into the night, making my workdays sixteen to seventeen hours.

My school days were Thursday through Saturday for eleven hours. On school days, if I was even one second late, I'd have to go home and make up my hours on an off day. On workdays, I was scheduled for 5:00 a.m. I was often late due to being so tired, and I did not have a car. I would borrow cars, catch rides, ride the bus, and call cabs to get around. Needless to say, I was exhausted. My boyfriend and I lived together, and because he got more irresponsible over time, even with my constant hustle, we were falling behind on bills.

I'd like to think one way God shows up is in our intuition. One particular day, Gerald was dropped off at home. Because neither of us had a car, we both could come home in a random vehicle on any given day, but this particular day, I got a bad feeling.

"So, when he came inside, I asked, "Who dropped you off?"

He responded, "Nikki."

I didn't have any reason to question him. Because of the age gap between Nikki and Gerald, I accepted his word about her being a mentor to him. I moved on, up until the night of the Dead Prez concert, which was promoted by Gerald and his partner. During the event, I went to use the restroom. When I came out of the stall, Nikki was standing there, waiting for me. I said, "Hello," and proceeded to wash my hands. She began to plead her case, sharing that nothing was going on between them. She told me Gerald was like a little brother to her, and she had an interest in painting a portrait of me. I was not trying to hear anything she had to say because I began the conversation about her role in Gerald's life with Gerald, not her. My relationship was not up for discussion with a third party. I just said, "Okay," and got the hell out of that bathroom as quickly as I could.

When I went back to my seat, I told Gerald what happened and asked him why Nikki felt the need to share those things with me.

He shrugged and said, "I don't know."

I then concluded that there was something going on between

them.

When we got home, I went about my nightly routine as usual and waited for Gerald to fall asleep. I grabbed his phone and went to his text message exchange with Nikki. I scrolled to the very beginning of the conversation thread and read everything. Their conversations made my uneasy feeling very clear. They were practically dating and probably gearing up for a relationship, if not already in one. I was in school thirty hours out of the week and working almost thirty to forty hours with my part-time job and braiding hair at home. Gerald had ample time to court Nikki. I already had a plan to wait out the last four months of our lease and then leave. Yet, after finding out about Nikki, there was no way I could continue to live with him.

We were behind one month on rent, and soon to be behind two months. Luckily for me, and thanks to Gerald for helping me to improve my interpersonal skills, I happened to maintain constant communication with our landlord. She knew all about his unwillingness to get a job, too, and she empathized with me. I let her know we were going to be late again with rent, and I asked her if we could break the lease. There were two weeks before we would have to pay rent, and she agreed to let us out of the lease with no fee as long as we were out within those two weeks.

Following my conversation with our landlord, when Gerald picked me up from work, I confronted him about the things I had seen on his phone. I informed him that I had gotten the landlord to break our lease since we were going to be late with rent again.

My last words were, "Wherever I go, you will not be going."

The car was silent all the way home. I had no clue where I'd go, but I knew I had to get away from him. Sometimes, you plant a seed and take a leap, even in the chaos, and God makes a way.

"A plan is not always needed. Sometimes, you need to just breathe, let go, and trust the universe."
— Unknown

I communed a lot with God during the later part of our relationship. I remember sobbing and asking God how I would get out of that situation. God gave me Nikki. And to think I had the evil eye towards her at first. Now, I'm grateful for her as I write this. She was a vessel. And God has a sense of humor, too, because years later, she was crushing on my now-husband while we were dating, and she was shocked when she saw me with him.

Gerald wasn't proud of what he had done and felt the least he could do was find me a place to live, so he asked his friend, GeeGee, if I could stay at her place. I probably only met GeeGee once, and I will forever be grateful to her and her roommate, Jenn, for allowing me to stay at their place. Jenn was away, since it was summer. She never met me and allowed me to sleep in her room while she was away. When she returned, I slept on the couch up to the point that the couch was sold because their lease was ending and they were selling the furniture. Both GeeGee and Jenn had graduated school, so they were moving out of that place to transition into their next phase of life. When the couch was gone, I slept on an armless chaise lounge. After about a month, the end of the lease grew closer, and I had no clue what to do.

To make matters worse, I was fired from my part-time job, and since I was not living in my own space, I was no longer styling at home. In retail, they have strict rules about lunch breaks, and I was one minute over before clocking out for my lunch break for the third time in six months, so my manager had to fire me. It took everything in me not to smile when she gave me the news. I hated that job from the moment I started. God knew I hated that place, and even in misery, I had no intentions of quitting, so the Most High handled the situation for me and got me out of there.

"God took care of me yesterday, took care of me today, and will take care of me tomorrow."
— Holley Gerth

I was happy to have been fired, but I had no clue what I would do for money or where I would live. I feel I have angels here on earth that God put here to make sure I'm always okay. It just so happened that through GeeGee, I met a woman around my grandmother's age whose house we would visit from time to time, and she'd cook for us. Gram Bee Bee is an amazing chef and baker, and she is so sweet and loving. When GeeGee's lease was up, Gram Bee Bee allowed us to live with her temporarily while we figured out our next steps.

The time neared for me and GeeGee to be moved out of Gram Bee Bee's place, and one day at school, I was sitting outside, alone, crying behind the back of the building. Cuyler, a classmate of mine, happened to pass by, and asked what was wrong. Typically, I was someone who would deal with hardship in silence and not share what I was struggling with, but something (God) led me to share with him that I was on the verge of being homeless and had no place to stay.

"Just because I carry it so well doesn't mean it's not heavy."
— Anonymous

I was distraught because I used to rarely cry no matter how hard things got, so if I shed tears, that meant things were really tough and I couldn't see a way out. Cuyler then shared with me a resource that was not public knowledge, which provided scholarship housing for students in need at my school. Although I was homeless and moving from one stranger's home to the next, the director had to be convinced that I was in need. I know I appeared fine on the outside at school. I'm sure that had a lot to do with it not being my first time in a homeless situation. I've had a blessed, yet tough, life. I don't carry what I've experienced, and I truly loved school because it allowed me to be in a place where I didn't have to focus on my troubles.

A part of me wonders why I had to convince the director that I needed help. We Black people, especially Black women, have a sense of pride in ourselves, keeping our heads high in the worst of situations, and I wonder if it was hard for the director to see my need for help because she was scoping my situation from a lack of cultural perspective. There was a four-bedroom, four-bathroom townhome being paid for that was created to help students in my situation, yet I had to convince her that I needed the assistance. She did ask if I had any family that could help. I had a couple of relatives in town. I only asked one of them, who had briefly lived with me previously, for help, though. They said I could live with them, but I had to pay rent and utilities, which I get, but I was jobless, so there's no way I could live with them with those stipulations. After repeatedly going into the director's office and giving her a letter highlighting my character, written by Gloria on my behalf, the director gave me the green light to move into the scholarship townhouse.

Before moving into the scholarship house, I recall having a conversation with Gram Bee Bee because GeeGee and I were in conversation about moving someplace together. I felt bad about finding myself a place to live and leaving GeeGee to fend for herself.

Gram Bee Bee looked me in the eye and said, "Charyl needs to do what's best for Charyl."

I knew I made the right decision.

"Never feel guilty for doing what's best for you."

Although I had to convince the director, I am very grateful that she decided to allow me to move into the scholarship home because she didn't owe me anything. My alma mater owed me nothing, too. I actually owed my school money. My tuition was supposed to be paid upfront. I was able to use the remaining financial aid available to me to pay my tuition; however, that didn't cover the total cost, so I had to take out a loan to cover the balance of my tuition. The agreement was that I had to make payments on the loan while enrolled, and the balance was to be fully paid by my graduation. I was fired from my job and was not styling hair, given my situation of being homeless, so there was no way I could continue making payments on my loan. My school was supposed to expel me, but because I was such a good student, I was allowed to stay in school and make the payments when I could. Looking back, I'm glad I kept the faith. Knowing the school's rules, I could've just outright given up, but I kept pushing, and God showed up for me.

God also showed up for me through my husband. After experiencing so much hurt in my past and being reluctant to date or entertain another man in my life, my husband, Cory, showed up as a reminder that I deserve to be loved.

The first time I met Cory was in the writing center. He was in conversation with my supervisor, showing her this painting he had done of Bob Marley. I pretended not to see him when I walked in. Somehow, we were introduced, and I remember giving him a card promoting my hair styling services. He had long locs at the time, and I must've been attracted to him because I was a novice with loc styling, and it was my least favorite thing to do. I was with Gerald, and Cory was actually kind of dating my coworker, so I didn't see him for a long time after that.

It was probably a year later when I met him again at a smoke shop where he worked. A classmate of mine was giving me a ride home, and she wanted to stop by the shop. While we were in the store, Cory talked to me the entire time. I was not the customer and I was not buying anything, but I got the customer service. I remember him smiling a lot. I'm sure I smiled a lot, too. When my classmate and I left the store, I paused at the door, closed my eyes, and put the question out into the universe: "What is this man's purpose in my life?" I recall reading an article once that stated if we put questions out into the universe, the answers will find us. I was still with Gerald; however, I knew he and I were done, and I was counting the days until our lease would end. Little did I know I would end the lease sooner than expected.

I was at school one day, and a classmate said to me for the third time or so that she had met a guy, and he reminded her so much of me to the point she felt he was the male version of me. The first time she shared this with me, I brushed her off because I felt she was just my classmate and didn't know me very well. What I didn't take into account is that my cosmetology classmates probably knew me better than any other classmates I'd ever had, being that we were in school for eleven hours and learned to perform our services on each other. Cosmetology students connect differently, so this time, when Terri mentioned to me that she'd met some guy who reminded her of me, Cory popped into my head.

I asked her, "Does he have long locs?"

She replied, "Yes."

I inquired, "Is his name Cory?"

Terri replied, "Yes."

I responded, "Oh, I know him," while wondering what the meaning of him, again, appearing in my life was.

The next time I saw Cory was when he came to do a tour at my school for the spa program. I gave him what he described to be a "church hug," and he shared with me that he was looking into the spa program. Because he gave me massage therapist vibes, I told him that was a good look for him. Before he left, I was sitting outside at a lunch table with my classmates, and he came to chat with me. Everyone at the table picked up on the chemistry between us. I was in denial.

Some time later, I attended Gerald's birthday party, even though we were broken up. I attended only because he wanted me there and to uphold the "everything is good between us, although we've broken up" campaign. Since Gerald was known by a lot of people, I didn't want to deal with people's inquiries about why we broke up. I even strategized not changing our Facebook statuses until three months after we had broken up. By the time our breakup was public knowledge, it was already old news.

When I got to the party, I had no interest in being around

Gerald or his friends. I spotted Cory, who was there doing a painting. To me, he was the most interesting person at the party, so I went and watched him paint. I was so fascinated by the portrait he was doing of Marvin Gaye. He was painting with Q-tips and wooden sticks that were the size of toothpicks. I thought he was purposely using those tools for texture purposes, and in conversation, I found out he had left his paintbrushes at home, which was literally up the street. He didn't want to go home and get the brushes, so he improvised. I was impressed. We conversed a bit, and there was a vibe between us. I noticed that a bug had flown into his cup of water, so I walked away to get him a new cup of water without telling him. When I returned to him with a fresh cup of water, unbeknownst to me at that time, Cory said to himself, "I'm going to make her my wife."

As planned, I only stayed at that party for an hour. I left without telling Cory that I was leaving. That night, he spent four hours in search of his old phone, so he could find the number that I had given to him via my business card way back when I first met him at the writing center. I got a random text from him either the following day or two days after the party. Somehow, that random message would turn into small talk here and there, and after maybe a few weeks of texting, I decided for us to finally hang out together. We did a painting together that came together so effortlessly that it looks like one person painted it. Cory was impressed. He had never painted with anyone, and his mind was blown at how well we worked together on the canvas. We started seeing each other frequently, and like the painting we created, we effortlessly became a couple.

Although I was reluctant, by the time I had graduated from cosmetology school, Cory and I were living together. When I expressed my hesitancy about us being together and living together, Cory said to me, "I won't say that I'm different from other guys, but I will say I'm better." I trusted his word, and we moved in together. By the time we moved in together, it was my sixth time moving in a six-month period.

When I graduated from cosmetology school, I had a tuition balance, so I was unable to take my state board exam and receive my license. Cory told me he'd help me. He took care of all of the bills while I worked and used my income to pay off my balance. I had applied to the salon that was next door and in connection to my cosmetology school. My educators worked at that salon, too. Working there was a way to gain experience and streamline into becoming an educator, which was my plan. Although I was hired, I was unable to work there without a license. I was hopeful, thinking that I would be able to work there because in Florida, an applicant preparing to take the state board exam could work under the supervision of a licensed cosmetologist, which is how cosmetology students can work on clients without licensing. I was hurt that the salon wouldn't allow me to work there while I worked towards paying my tuition balance. My thought was, How will I pay my tuition balance to get my license if I'm not working?

Luckily for me, I found a nail salon that allowed me to work there while I worked towards positioning myself to take my state board exam. Everything happens as it should, too, because I'd end up meeting one of my closest friends while working at that nail salon.

It was no small feat, yet, with the work I put in at the nail salon, I finally paid off the remaining balance of my tuition. The loan officer was so proud of me. He said most people in my situation never paid. A stern email he sent also played a role in my determination to pay my balance. There was a time after graduation when I made more excuses than payments, and once the loan officer called me out, I got laser-focused. I appreciate him for that "get your life together" moment. After strategically studying to refresh everything I had learned in school, I scheduled my state board exam, and I passed with flying colors.

I realized that my Asian employers favored their white customers over their Black customers, and since hair styling was my passion, I decided to find a job as a stylist. What I should've done prior to applying to Save-A-Dollar Salon was a day of shadowing; it was a good start for experience; however, working there revealed that I deserve better.

I did better for myself by getting out of the salon tucked in the corner of the department store by the bathrooms and into a new salon in Midtown, targeting a more affluent clientele. As it turns out, a salon can be in a better location and still have the morale of the gutter.

In the beginning, I don't recall having any bad feelings about Venue Salon; however, I noticed that it was kind of the upgraded version of where I came from, with a similar culture of low morale. Although very talented, the owner, Allison, spoke negatively about people a lot—so much that a coworker of mine had anxiety, fearing that when she wasn't around, Allison spoke badly of her.

I'm not sure if it was solely the work environment or a combination of personal life and work life; however, two of the employees at Venue Salon told me that they were on depression medicine. I thought everyone else's mood and conditions would not affect me. What I did not know is that I am an empath. I was definitely affected by the energy around me and later found myself feeling depressed.

I talked to the owner about leaving. We decided I would cut my hours instead. I still felt uneasy. One day, I showed up to work and felt that I was talked about before I stepped into the room. I chose to be the bigger person and greeted everyone. Allison chose to turn her body in a direction to not have to speak to me. I made a decision.

While everyone else was preparing their stations for their incoming clients, I went outside to my car, pulled it up to the back door, and went back inside to my workstation. I packed up all of my things in a big black garbage bag, took the garbage bag outside to my car, put it in the backseat, and left. I was done.

"If you allow people to make more withdrawals than deposits in your life, you will be out of balance and in the negative. Know when to close the account."
— Christie Williams

While working at the salon, there was a skincare and waxing business I frequented for about eight years, and I had developed a friendship with Jacqueline, the owner. One day, during a service, while I was lying on the table, she asked me if I ever thought about doing eyelash extensions. It is something that I thought about doing, especially after finding out that her believable eyelashes were faux mink extensions. After that conversation, Jacqueline connected me to my first lash trainer, who had twenty years' experience. She was so impressed by my natural knack for applying eyelash extensions that she tried to hire me. I figured I had a knack for eyelash application because of the dexterity in my fingers as a braider. Once certified, I started working for Jacqueline part-time, and I was still at Venue Salon part-time, until the day when I packed up and left.

Being a lash artist was tough; it took me two years to build a steady clientele. I got a part-time job to have an income while I worked on building my clientele. At the beginning of my lash career, I felt supported by Jacqueline. She paid for my lash training and allowed me to pay her back in increments. She didn't have to do that. However, with perspective, I understand now that what she did for me was also of direct benefit to her.

What was great, in the beginning, is I felt like I worked for myself. The workspace she and I shared was not large enough for the two of us to work simultaneously. I enjoyed being able to work in peace. At first, there was a lot of peace because I didn't have many clients. I underwent a lesson in manifestation because Jacqueline suggested that I still show up and report to work even if there was no one on the schedule, which would be my way of communicating to the universe that I wanted to be booked and busy during that time.

"To manifest, act as if."
— Unknown

On days when I didn't have clients, I practiced lash application, washed and folded towels, and used that time to market on social media. I was very serious about being successful. Most people had no idea that the service existed or what it entailed, so that meant I had to work overtime with my service promotion if I wanted to be successful.

In the beginning, there were little signs that I would have to compromise myself and bend to coexist with Jacqueline at Five Star Spa. I noticed them, but I didn't take the time to evaluate what they meant.

"Listen to the universe. It's always whispering messages."
— Unknown

After two years of alternating workdays and sharing one room, Jacqueline purchased a business space. The transition was a hectic, yet exciting time. I'm learning to honor my intuition more because as we transitioned to the new space, I had a feeling that things would shift towards the worse.

"Trust your intuition. It speaks softly. But when you listen, the message is always clear."
— Mindful Marketplace

Jacqueline and I worked hard; we had a lot of fun together and learned a lot from each other. She and I laid out our relationship and communication style on a growing document that was facilitated by this couple who trademarked a system for building and maintaining healthy relationships. The document worked well until it was disregarded. In close relationships of close quarters, if we're not careful, we can project our insecurities and negative feelings onto the people closest to us, which is why it is imperative to always be in touch with ourselves and always work on elevating. Because of stress, I uncoupled from my long-term boyfriend, my now-husband, because I took my stress out on our relationship. The actual problem was me being overworked, and I did not have the time or energy to be present in the relationship. However, I see purpose in our separation because it helped me see that my job was a huge part of the problem.

Initially, I was treated as a business partner. I have a

Bachelor of Science degree in Public Relations, and I shared my knowledge with Jacqueline as she shared her knowledge of skincare, waxing, and business with me. I connected her to a friend who is a graphic designer, who helped her with branding. I wrote and edited the website copy for the business. I drafted the press release for our grand opening. I set up a meeting with a former professor to receive insight into the planning of the grand opening. I recorded key moments of the grand opening for social media. In hindsight, I should've honored my expertise by being paid for my PR work. However, I was inexperienced in the aspect of offering freelance PR services, and I was just glad to help the business be successful. Furthermore, Jacqueline and I both interviewed potential team members. We hired each person in agreement.

In my early days at Five Star Spa, one of my former professors, who was also my client and friend, said to me, "This is nice and all, but don't get stuck here." Gram Bee Bee never met Jacqueline, and she said the same thing to me. I made a mental note of their advice. I should've sat with their words. They saw something that I didn't. I never intended to work for Jacqueline forever, although she would've loved that because she said so. She told me that after five years, she'd give me ten percent of her business. I remember asking myself, *Why would I want 10 percent of her business when I can have 100 percent of my own?* I understand now that what my professor and Gram Bee Bee were saying to me is that God has bigger plans for my life.

"God's plans will always be greater and more beautiful than all your disappointments."
— hubpages.com

In the new space, I went from working an eight-hour work shift to a ten-hour work shift with no lunch break. We couldn't have a lunch break between 11:00 a.m. and 3:00 p.m. because those were our peak business hours. I remember I was so burnt out, and one of Jaqueline's best friends, who would come to me for services, told me that if I needed a break, I should take it. I switched my schedule to 9:00 a.m. to 3:00 p.m., then returned from 5:00 p.m. to 7:00 p.m. for evening clients who couldn't come during the day. That window went away soon because Jacqueline asked for favors during my break window, and those favors would include client services, so I went back to working from 9:00 a.m. to 7:00 p.m.

While venting to a client about my experiences, she suggested the book *Working While Black* and told me about the hashtag #blackwomenatwork. From the hashtag, I discovered the term "microaggressions." Reviewing the tweets and the Facebook posts from Black women all over the country, I realized I wasn't alone in my experience, being the only Black team member. I didn't want the position, but Jacqueline gave me the responsibility of being a team leader. She told me I would have a pay increase, and I never did receive the increase.

"Leadership is not wielding authority—it is empowering people."
— Becky Brodin

There's winning, and then there's learning. What I gathered from my work experience is that my relationship with Jacqueline was just a reflection of all of my relationships, be they familial, romantic, or platonic. No matter the relationship, my role was always to please people and put the feelings of others before my own. Now, I know if my compassion doesn't start with me, I am not doing it right. God didn't send me here to suffer. And although, as a highly sensitive person, I am internally disturbed and affected by conflict, I've learned that conflict is okay when it comes to self-advocating, and I have to stand up for myself no matter what.

"Your silence gives consent."
— Plato

I learned from experience to never put the consideration of others before me. One morning, before my work shift, Cory and I headed to a car repair shop. My car was serviced the day before, and someone broke something on my car, so we were going to find out what happened. The road was wet, so as we approached the light, to be careful, Cory stopped a whole car length and then some away from the car in front of us. A feeling came over me.

I yelled, "Oh, shit!"

Cory questioned, "What? I'm at a complete stop."

Immediately after, a car crashed into the back of us, pushing us into the car in front of us. The car that rear-ended us bounced back and hit the car behind her. Then, the driver spun out and hit a car in the lane on her right. When all of the crashes were over and everyone stepped out of their cars confused, trying to figure out what happened, we realized we had been in a five-car collision. My car was totaled.

While we stood around waiting for the police report and insurance information, I thought about the full book of clients I had, so I called Jacqueline and told her I was in a collision. Her response was, "There's no reason you can't come to work today." As the "go along to get along girl," I agreed to go to work until the adrenaline faded and my body stiffened from whiplash. I contacted her and told her I could not come to work. I thought she'd inform my clients and just reschedule them. She spread out my eyebrow-shaping clients onto everyone else's schedules and rescheduled the lash clients because no one could do their services but me.

That day would be the second accident I experienced within six months. The first accident happened right after I had dropped Cory to work. I had more than enough time to get to work myself, but in my head, I was rushing. My work experience was a catalyst for anxiety. The light changed for oncoming traffic. I had ample time to pull out, but because I was rushing in my head, I pulled out onto Thomasville Road kind of fast. I straightened up, or I thought I did; then, it felt like a brush of wind came beneath my back tires, and my car started spinning. The last thing I remember seeing before I pulled out was a semi-truck, so as my car spun, I closed my eyes and prepared to die.

What stopped me was my car crashing parallel into the side of another car, and I laughed as I had the thought, *You thought you were getting off that easy?* From anxiety and depression, I had been experiencing suicidal thoughts, which is why I was so accepting of death as my car spun. But it was made clear that I still have a purpose.

I contacted Jacqueline about my collision and let her know that my car wasn't drivable. She sent the receptionist to pick me up. I left my car in the parking lot and went to work. Since I showed up to work after the first collision, I could see how I set the tone for her, six months later, to say there was no reason for me not to be at work.

"Be careful what you tolerate. You are teaching people how to treat you."
—- Lindsay Walden

I went to work the day after the five-car collision. I was an hour late because the car rental place had no available cars as a result of many collisions and a car recall. I was there for hours trying to get a car, and I was in communication with my first client the entire time. Although the rental car situation cut into my client's appointment, I had substantial time to do her service. From experience, I learned to allot extra time on the schedule for first-time lash clients. Cory reached out to a manager he knew, and that's how I finally got a rental car.

Once in, I went through the intake form with her, as I did with every client. When I was done with her service, she loved her lashes, but I felt bad about being late, so I told her to come back the next morning, and I'd add more lashes to her set during a thirty-minute window.

The following day, I was running behind. My body was still recovering from the collision. I messaged her to let her know I'd be five minutes late. I was two minutes late and beat her coming in. Again, she was happy with the result of her lashes. The following day, she left me a three-star review on Yelp, saying I was very educated about my craft and did well, but I was late. She didn't lie; however, she left out context. I was upset because Jacqueline was often late and had never received one bad review. The client was in her twenties and Hispanic. I felt that because I was a Black woman, I was not extended any grace.

It wasn't our first time receiving a bad review, so I crafted a response in Jacqueline's voice. She liked it, but the following day, she posted a different response and planned to send the client free products. The day after, I showed up to work and saw that a souvenir makeup bag from the lash company I was an ambassador for was missing from my room. I asked the receptionist if she knew what happened to my bag. She looked afraid and scarily said something about Jacqueline taking it. I quickly marched into Jacqueline's room, ready to snap, but decided I didn't want to appear like the angry Black woman, so I took the peaceful approach and asked about my bag. She had placed the free products for the three-star review client in my bag and sent them to her. I think I walked outside to cool off, and I ended up sending her a message in Slack, a platform I introduced her to for team and project management. She said that she would order me a new bag, and I calmed down.

Sometime later, the replacement bag arrived, and it was smaller and cheaply made in comparison. Jacqueline was away. I sent her a message, letting her know what she did was not okay. I didn't let up until she admitted to wrongdoing, which was unheard of. So, when she returned, I was berated in a three-hour meeting, during which she deemed that the situation was my fault. She said I should've caught an Uber to work instead of getting a rental car. I was in the rental car for a month, too, because that's how long it took for me to find a new car. In that three-hour meeting, I determined I was done, and I'd never again overextend myself for a client.

"You'll know when you're done."
— My Mom

I no longer broke my back to make sure the business ran smoothly. I went into a crystal shop one day. Something drew me towards a particular stone that had "harmony" etched on it. I placed the crystal inside my workroom, not knowing that black crystals are protective stones. It wasn't long after placing that stone in my room that I left Five Star Spa. The stone represented my prayer for harmony with the divine plan for my life, and now, it's a part of my testimony. I see testimony as a test of harmony with God's will. Working there was no longer good for me, but I didn't have a plan B or the energy to come up with one. Plan B showed up in the form of a chemical allergy.

Trying to figure out what irritated my eyes, I went back and forth to the eye doctor, with no medical insurance, for months before I figured out it was the lash adhesive. I didn't wear extensions; it was the invisible fumes that I reacted to from breathing them in. I had an inflamed cornea and tiny bumps under my eyelids. My closet-sized room was too small of a workspace for me to be applying lashes. I learned that my room should've been the largest and most ventilated room in the building. When I first noticed that something was going on with me and the adhesive, I told Jacqueline. For whatever reason, she didn't respond to what was happening with me until it was too late.

I think my allergy was the result of a combination of overexposure to the fumes (working ten hours), poor ventilation (closet-sized room), poor eating habits (no lunch breaks), stress (overworked), and a lack of self-love. I'm fearfully and wonderfully made (Psalm 139:13–14), and I simply was not holding reverence for myself during this period of my life. My body's initial response to the adhesive fumes was itchy eyes. Next, I started experiencing a pins-and-needles type of itchiness all over my body, from my head to the bottoms of my feet and in my throat. Once I was clear about being allergic to the adhesive, I called Jacqueline, who was out of town, to let her know. She responded that I still had to work.

And, like a woman out of touch with her self-worth, I continued to work. Because I was told I had to work, I exposed myself to the lash adhesive for two weeks. Each day, the allergy worsened. Initially, I was fine for most of my workday, and the itchy pins-and-needles feeling came towards the end of my shift. Then, my symptoms started at the beginning of my workday and persisted until the time I went to sleep.

I couldn't suffer any longer. I showed up to work with a full schedule, booked out for months, and told the receptionist, "I'm not taking any more lash appointments." It felt good to take my power back, but I felt bad for my lash clients. I had signs that I was sensitive to the eyelash adhesive for months, and it would have been best to communicate that from the start. I have no idea what Jacqueline said to my clients, and the lash artist that she recommended to them was subpar simply because she was a beginner. A part of me wonders if they were upset with me for how things turned out, but Five Star Spa wasn't my business. I did my best, given the situation.

After working at Five Star Spa, I was burnt out and unsure if I wanted to continue in the beauty industry. After a few months, I rented a vacant room to offer the services I could. I sent Jacqueline a courtesy email about my plans. I thought it was best that she received the information from me. Little did I know that she'd do everything in her power for me not to succeed. She purposely disturbed my peace, and I should've continued to brush it off and pray for her.

"Bless your enemy and rob them of ammunition."
— Florence Scovel Shinn (The Game of Life and How to Play It)

Instead, I fed into the mess. Initially, I had no intentions of poaching clients I served at Five Star Spa because I wanted a fresh start. One of the clients I texted was a die-hard Five Star customer, and I found out later that she had shown Jacqueline my text messages, which influenced her to come after me more. I worked in the space I rented for six months. The owner decided to give the room to her best friend. We had no contract, so there was nothing I could do but move out.

It took six months before I tried working in the beauty industry again. I later met two wonderful women: one whom I spent six months working for until I realized that the chemical in lash adhesive is also in nail products; and the other, who would provide a room for me to rent during the COVID-19 pandemic once I decided to try to offer services that I could perform (like eyebrow shaping and tinting).

After six months, I decided that renting the space wasn't the best decision. I had come to learn that the chemical I'm allergic to is not only in all beauty products, but also in fragrances, hand sanitizers, cigarette smoke, dry erase markers, and the list goes on. Leaving my home puts me at risk of experiencing my chest tightening, trouble breathing, itchy and bloodshot red eyes, an itchy throat, an itchy body, chronic fatigue, and brain fog. The chemical affects my nervous system, so I stutter sometimes, too. Fragrance allergies are considered an invisible disability, and like all disabilities, it affects my quality of life.

Even with my health condition and experiences in the beauty industry, I've still found it in me to continue my passion for helping women feel confident through affordable and stylish jewelry from my online boutique. I suffered more than I had to because of my stubbornness to stick to my plan. There were signs and an inner knowing that I deserved better, and I didn't honor myself. Now, I'm more intentional with my relationship with the Most High because God's plan is always better.

Before the allergy, I was in Atlanta for a lash training, and I visited Gloria to catch up. I shared that I was recently certified to microblade. She was impressed that I added another skill to my repertoire.

She asked, "So, what's next?"

I paused to think about it and replied, "I want to write."

I had no idea how that would come to be; years later, here

I am.

"Life tried to crush her, but only succeeded in creating a diamond."
— John Mark Green

Charyl M. Williams

Chapter 6

A Victim Turned Warrior Queen

The Beginning

Milwaukee, Wisconsin is all I ever knew in my early adolescent years. All of my immediate family resided there, and it was the place I was born and raised in, initially. Growing up with a teenage mother and a nonexistent biological father caused me to grow up quicker than most kids.

I always felt the emptiness of my father not being present. My mother had me at fifteen years old and my twin brother and sister by the age of nineteen. I was always searching for a dad, although I called my grandfather "Daddy." His logic was that he was too young to be called Grandpa. Hilarious, right? But he was still my grandfather, yet also a father figure in my life. Nevertheless, I was very aware of the difference between a grandfather and a biological father. I even turned to my brother's and sister's dad and began calling him "Daddy," but then, he and my mother didn't work out. Once again, I was a little four-year-old girl longing for a daddy.

Then came along my ex-stepfather. I was six years old, and I distinctly remember telling my mother that I wanted to call him "Daddy." She was apprehensive at first, but then obliged to me calling him that. I finally felt like I would have that father-daughter relationship I always yearned for and saw between my friends and their dads. I was the flower girl at their wedding and had high hopes of being a "Daddy's girl."

We stayed in Milwaukee for a few more years until I turned ten years old. Little did I know this man was a narcissist and would move me and my mother away from my family to Atlanta, Georgia, only for his true intentions to be to isolate us from our family. He stated it was God that told him to move, but as time went on, my mom and I found that to be untrue.

Truth be told, on the onset, I was excited to move to the big A-T-L. Everyone in Milwaukee used to talk about Atlanta. When my friends got word of me moving, they acted as if it was the best thing in the world. "Girl, you moving to Atlanta, you moving to A-T-L!" It was a major thing on my block for me to be moving.

It doesn't hit me until my mother and I are at the gate and it's time for me and her to kiss my Suga Mama, my grandma, goodbye. *Wait, we're really leaving*, I begin to think to myself. My Suga Mama helped raise me; I saw her almost every day. No more seeing her. My brother and sister are with their granny and will join us later. We're moving thousands of miles away. No friends, no family, just me, my mom, and him.

So many emotions were going through my ten-year-old head at the time. This was before 9/11, so family and friends were still allowed to come through TSA and wait at the gate with you. As we begin boarding the plane, I look back at my Suga Mama, and tears begin rolling down my and my mother's faces. The further we walk, the more distant her face becomes. We enter the plane and take our seats. I look out the window, and life as I know it—all my friends, all the memories, all of my family—is no longer my normal. I'm about to enter a city I know nothing about, and I know absolutely no one.

Darkness in the Shadows

It's late Friday evening, and I am laying with my eyes closed in my nightgown. The subdivision outside light is beaming into my room, just enough light so that my room isn't pitch black. I'm still afraid of the dark, so this is the perfect night light. I'm laying there, barely able to fall asleep, yet I keep trying to doze off. My mind just won't relax. I'm lying in my bed missing my Suga Mama, family, and friends back home in Milwaukee. Suga Mama is the beat to my heartbeat, my everything. *Why did we have to move to this state? Why Georgia, away from all of my family and my brother and sister?* I begin to think to myself. My new normal is a constant struggle, and night after night, I battle getting rest.

Finally, I fall asleep, when I hear my door opening with

a screech. But this time, it's not the normal sound of the door opening; it's as if someone is creeping into my room. I immediately lock up, and close my eyes tight. Wait, am I dreaming or awake? I begin to think to myself.

Suddenly, a body slowly lies in my bed next to me. My eyes are locked shut, but my sense of smell is heightened. I know this scent and this body, though, yet he's being quiet. This is weird. My young intuition can feel something is off, so I don't move or say a word. I know something is not right about this situation. He then gets in the bed and proceeds to lay behind me, and I feel something hard pressing up against me, pushing up against my gown. *WHAT IS GOING ON?* I think to myself. *Wait. Why is he doing this to me? Why is he in here? Why can I feel his private area; why is it hard?*

He proceeds to move his body back and forth, slowly hunching behind me even more... *Girl, snap out of it,* I think to myself. *This has to be a nightmare! Scream! Scream, for God's sake, so your mom knows what is going on.* My mind is racing, yet my body is numb. I'm stuck, I can't move, I can barely breathe. Paralysis enters my body from head to toe. Then, before I know it, the worst part happens. He proceeds to slowly go into my underwear. Maybe if I move a little, it'll make him stop. Adjusting my body slightly, I move towards the edge of the bed. Instead of stopping, he presses his body firmly up against mine and moves towards the end of the bed with me. *Surely, he thinks I am asleep, but please, make him stop. God, help me! Stop him, please. This isn't right. This is disgusting.* I feel so dirty, embarrassed, ashamed, and humiliated, yet I still can't bring myself to move not even an inch anymore. I can't bring myself to fight this man off of me. He proceeds to move his hands inside of my panties. I mentally go into a dark hole and just accept this is happening to me and there's nothing I can do.

What felt like a lifetime slowly comes to an end as he gradually pulls his hands out of my panties, eases his way out of my bed, gently closes the door, and proceeds to go back into his room with my mother. As I'm laying there, tears begin to fall from my eyes, yet my eyes are still shut, mouth glued shut, while my body sinks into the bed. A few minutes pass by, and I'm still stuck in the same spot when I begin to hear the noises. *I know that's not what I think I'm hearing.* He came in, molested me, and immediately went back to wake my mother up and have sex with her.

I laid in my bed, paralyzed for what felt like a century, frozen, more tears rushing down my face. I couldn't believe what had just happened. *WHY ME?* Little did I know this was just the beginning of my INNOCENCE BEING SNATCHED from me by a man who was supposed to be my stepfather. I was supposed to be a "Daddy's girl." Why would he do this to me? From this day forward, I knew my life would never be the same. I was living with who most would consider—and from that day forward, who I considered as—"the Bogeyman." My mother had no idea she married a monster and I was his main victim, yet, I wasn't brave enough to tell her. I became a prisoner in my own body from that day forward.

The next morning, my mother is getting ready to run her normal errands, when she comes into my room and says, "Make sure you make your bed and come eat." I slowly sit up, get out of the bed, and can barely move my feet. The feeling of pure filth, lowness, and dirtiness consumes all of me, yet I still can't bring myself to tell her what happened to her eleven-year-old eldest daughter. *Just tell her!* I think to myself. As I finish making my bed, I proceed to walk out of my bedroom door, and here comes the Bogeyman, coming out of his and my mother's room at the same time as me. A flashback of the noises from last night entered my mind.

"Morning."

I ignore him and walk straight into the bathroom. He acts as if everything is normal.

"You don't hear me talking to you?"

"Good morning," I mumble under my breath.

"Here she goes again, being disrespectful with that

attitude," he quickly says to my mother.

"Speak when Daddy is talking to you," she tells me.

Are you kidding me? You have no idea who you married! I think to myself.

"Okay, Ma. I didn't hear him."

I can't fathom the sight or sound of him, so I quickly close the door, run the water from the sink, and look at myself in the mirror. The first thought to my head is, *Girl, you'll be better off dead.* Life as I knew it through my precious, innocent eyes no longer looked the same. *This has to be a nightmare; this has to be hell*, I begin to think to myself. There's a knock on the door.

"I'm about to go. You can stay with Daddy," she says, but what I hear is, "You can stay with the Bogeyman."

"No, Ma. I'm going to go with you."

I'll be back. Just stay here with Daddy."

This man is not my daddy; he's not my stepfather. He's a monster, and I need to leave with my mom so I can tell her, I think to myself, yet that doesn't happen. I freeze again and do as I am told.

You're stupid. You can't even speak up for yourself, I say to myself. Watching my mom leave the apartment, her footsteps, one by one, become more faint. She turns and says, "I love you." Then, she's gone. I'm left in this apartment by myself with this monster. *Let me just stay busy. Go clean your room, eat breakfast—whatever you do, don't end up next to him.* I walk back into the bathroom and begin running my bathwater. I can still smell his scent on me. I scrub my body until my skin turns red. I'm crying, asking God why He let this happen to me. This would be the beginning of my depression setting in and the suicidal thoughts beginning to affect me tremendously. I just wanted to die. I quickly dry off and get dressed so I can eat my breakfast.

I finish my cereal, go to my room, and BOOM—the flashbacks from just short of a few hours ago begin to revisit my mind. It's so clear, it's as if it's happening to me at that moment. I'm standing in my room and a burst of tears begin falling down my face. Then, suddenly, there's another knock at my door. I jump up with such fear that my tears instantly dry.

"Yes?"

"Come out here and watch this movie with me."

"I'm cleaning my room right now. I'll be out in a bit."

"Well, why is your room door locked? I know you're not in there doing something you're not supposed to be doing."

"No, I am not. I must have pushed the button by accident."

"Well, open the door."

I am trembling, eyes dazed in fear, heart racing to the point it feels as if it's about to jump through my shirt.

"Okay. Changing my shirt."

"What are you doing?" he asks.

"I am just changing my shirt, Da… Daddy." I could barely call him that.

He walks away. I change my shirt, open the door, and proceed to go to the living room to watch the movie.

That Friday evening was the beginning of me living in what felt like hell. The sexual abuse went on for about three and a half years. Oftentimes, I would be scared to sleep in the bed by myself, so although I would not want to lay by him, I would still hop in the bed with him and my mother. He would be in the middle, with me on one side and my mother on the other. As any father would do, he would hold me, but it wasn't your normal father-and-daughter hold. As my mother laid on the other side of us, not knowing a thing, he would become erect behind me. I still didn't say a word. I was too scared to. I was too scared to sleep by myself, so again, I blamed myself for what was happening to me. This period of my life sparked so many feelings of emptiness from not having my

116

biological father. I yearned for the protection and presence from my real dad. Maybe if he was in my life, this would not have happened to me.

I could not tell anyone. I went to school and saw all my friends with their fathers, while I had one in my life who was supposed to be my dad, but took advantage of me. *What the heck was wrong with me? Why couldn't I be loved and wanted properly by my real father?* was a consistent thought in my head. I did have my grandfather, but he was thousands of miles away.

So, here I am in Stone Mountain, Georgia, with no family. My brother and sister are still in Milwaukee at the time, and I am down here with my mother and this monster. I had no outlets.

My Suga Mama (my grandmother) was my best friend, yet I couldn't bring myself to tell her, either. The effects of being molested as an innocent child spilled into my character as a little girl. Anger and rage were constant feelings. My grades never slipped in school, but the anger came out during confrontations in school. Somehow, I was still able to talk my way out without getting suspended. That was the mini lawyer in me.

I soon began to discover the power of poetry, and this became my outlet to release my emotions. But still, there was emptiness within from the effects of the ongoing sexual and emotional trauma, along with my biological father not being present. So, what does a young girl do when she is not being shown proper love by a man? She seeks out the attention from young boys. I fell prey to young boys and leaned into them to fill the void that should have been given by my father. A mastery of smiles and facades of being "okay" was second nature to me, when deep down, I had so much darkness within. I was depressed and would cut myself with a little razor in places no one would see to help cope with the pain.

As I wrote my poems, I would tap into every emotion I was feeling. One particular poem was called *Heaven or Hell?* It was during a Christmas visit to Milwaukee, Wisconsin. We are in the living room, and my Suga Mama asks me to read some of my new poems. So, I choose that poem to read aloud, and as I am reading, my Suga Mama looks over to my mom and makes a face.

Once I'm finished, she says, "What made you write this poem?"

I look at her and say, "Do you really have a choice if you live through a life of hell?"

She looks at me in disbelief, looks over to my mom, and says, "What's going on?"

My mother had no words because she did not know, either.

Quickly pivoting the conversation, I say, "Well I saw a movie and pulled from there as inspiration."

I lied. I mean, I had to—there was no way I could tell my Suga Mama or mother why I really wrote the poem. I had no idea how to explain or tell my family what my stepfather was doing to me. I blamed myself and thought I deserved it. I didn't know how to say how much I needed my biological father. Feeling alone became my norm. So, as always, I just covered the truth and did not say anything.

At the time, poetry and my little boyfriend were my way of escaping my reality. Although my mother did not condone me having a boyfriend in middle school, I didn't care. I became resentful towards her and did what I wanted to do. I began blaming her for what happened to me and questioning why she didn't know.

Growing Up Too Fast

Living in Georgia made me grow up fast. I hung out with the older kids, lied about my age, and thought I was grown. Being touched at such a young age changes you; it makes you view life differently. *If he could touch me in that way, then maybe I am mature enough to do this or do that...* That was my attitude. So, I ended up getting myself in a situation where I almost found myself repeating history over again.

As I mentioned, my mother had me at fifteen years old, and from the time of birth, many had already said I would follow right behind her. So, at the age of fourteen, I had my first "puppy love" boyfriend. I really thought I loved him, so I chose to attempt to have sex.

My childhood best friend and I were having a conversation about virginity, and she expressed to me that I should wait, but I wasn't hearing that. I thought I loved him. So, I told her I was going to do it. He was telling me everything I needed to hear and filling a void, so I thought. Thankfully, I didn't get pregnant, and we didn't go all the way through, but yet again, I was chasing something through a male due to the deeper-rooted issues and demons I was fighting.

Throughout my journey in middle and high school, my relationship with my mother became very combative and distant, with lots of arguing, talking back, and resentment. We bumped heads a lot, and by the time my brother and sister moved down to Georgia permanently, I felt like I received the short end of the stick in the way she disciplined me compared to them. It felt as if she was always trying to make up for the time they did not live with us, but as a result, I felt as if we were treated differently. I was always the child with the attitude, acting too grown, but they could do no wrong.

By the time I was going into the ninth grade, my stepfather had walked out on us. I was so happy he was finally gone. My mom's male friend had come around to help us. *My brother and sister are living with us, and this monster is finally gone, so I guess I should be happy*, I thought. *But still, that little girl within is hurting, broken, empty, and buried with so much pain inside.* Depression, low self-worth, and the constant desire to die are feelings I just couldn't seem to shake. Yet, I hid everything. I internalized my feelings and just went on day by day, needing to be saved. I was just a little girl who was shattered and humiliated by the sexual abuse I had to endure. I felt like a victim, embarrassed and ashamed that I couldn't speak up.

My view of men was warped. *I hate my life, but maybe him leaving will make things better*, I thought. Boy was I wrong, because deep down, I had no idea what would lie ahead of me when it came to drowning in my misery.

The Tell

My mother's male friend ended up moving in with us not long after my stepfather left, and he was helping us out. He and I had an okay relationship. I looked at him more like an older brother. Nonetheless, I still could not understand how or why my mother would want him to stay with us. I mean, he and I had a pretty good relationship, but after what I had been through, I did not want another man living with us.

The weight of the molestation became unbearable. One day during my freshman year, I ended up asking him, "What would you tell someone to do if they've been touched by someone?"

It caught him by surprise, and he said, "They should definitely speak up regarding it."

That particular conversation is a blur because I mentally blacked out. I could not believe I even asked him that… It then prompted him to go to my mom about the question, and my mother approached me about it. I was scared to speak about it, but I finally coughed up the courage and told her that my stepfather molested me… At this time, I had not told her the full details of what happened and how long it had taken place, but my truth was finally out of the bag.

Attempting to End My Life

It's my tenth-grade year, and I'm on the phone with my boyfriend. My mother and I had just finished arguing about her boyfriend, and how I was being disrespectful. It was an ongoing cycle between us. The arguments and bumping of heads were getting worse. Hearing her talking on the phone with my grandmother about my attitude, some of her outlooks were valid regarding my attitude, but she never considered how I felt regarding her boyfriend moving in with us just a year prior. I was pissed that the friend then became her boyfriend and quickly moved in with us right after my ex-stepfather left. I was sick of a man living with us and letting me down. I was tired of a man not really being what I needed as a teenager. The little girl within was still suffering, and after telling my mother about the situation between me and my stepfather, I just needed space from any man being around. But Mom had to have a life, too, right? That's not how I saw it. I felt like she should have protected me more emotionally in the moment of finding out I was sexually abused, and I felt like that protection should have included not having another man living in our home.

I was a ticking time bomb, brewing with hatred and disgust. I wasn't shown what it looked like to be treated properly by a man. My ex-stepfather had a temper. He would hit things in our apartments and verbally abuse my mother, and he was sexually and emotionally abusive to me. Then, my biological father was not in the picture, so my view of men was tainted, and I was distrustful of them. Yet, I was still in search of a boy to fill the void from the absence of my father and the mistrust from my ex-stepfather.

As I'm on the phone with my boyfriend, I tell him, "I'm done. I can't do this anymore! Life isn't worth living!"

The bottle of pills is next to my bed, and my door is closed. I reach over and pop a little over fifteen pills. I lost count. You can hear the fear in his voice as he hears me taking the pills. He tried to talk me out of it, but I wasn't hearing it. Quickly hanging up, he calls my mother and tells her I just took pills to kill myself.

I needed to numb the pain. I needed to rest! I needed the thoughts in my mind to stop racing. The pills were the only thing I felt to be my release.

I slowly begin drifting off, losing consciousness, when my mother bursts in the door and screams, "Did you take pills?!"

My eyes drift closed and I'm out. Next, I remember being in the hospital room, hooked up with an IV and the heart monitor sounding excruciatingly loud.

I vaguely hear my mom saying, "She tried to kill herself and took pills."

"How many pills, ma'am?"

The heart monitor begins to slow down. *Lord, please just take me now*, I think in my head. I'm drifting in and out of consciousness. My mother is crying, and all I can think is, *God, please take me now*. My recollection becomes faint, but I remember someone coming in and saying, "We may need to pump her stomach." They try to wake me up, and as I'm barely able to open my eyes, they hand me a cup filled with what looks like tar. The substance is dark brown, thick, and smells like a sour, spoiled smoothie.

"You need to drink the whole cup, or you're going to have to get your stomach pumped."

Still going in and out, the cup is held to my mouth, and I begin to swallow. *This is not how this was supposed to go.* After being forced to drink the charcoal, another person comes in and begins asking me a series of questions.

One question was "Did you take pills to kill yourself?"

"No. I just wanted to rest and numb my pain."

Well, little did I know, answering it as such would cause me to be admitted to a psychiatric hospital. Apparently, based on my response, since I did not admit to wanting to commit suicide, I was going to need to be admitted. *Just great, these folks are acting like I'm crazy. I hate that feeling. If only they knew what I've been through. I can't confess it aloud, though. If I tell them what happened to me, what would people think about my mother?* Plus, I didn't want Georgia's Division of Family and Children Services (DCFS) to get involved.

I lay in the bed feeling so defeated, still hooked up to an IV, the bitter aftertaste of the charcoal mixture in my mouth, thinking to myself, *Why did my life have to turn out like this?* I look over and see my mother sleeping, and tears begin rolling down my face. It's just me in this dark hospital room, the sky is dark, and barely any light is shining into the room. I begin thinking about the failed relationships; not having my biological father; being away from my family; missing my Suga Mama; replaying the nights of being molested, all the poems I wrote to release, the constant arguing with my mother, and how her not understanding that bringing a man in the house after my stepfather left was the worst timing for me… just wanting to die! I hate my life. I hate that I can't express this out loud. I hate that everything between my mother and I is always that I "have an attitude," or I'm "being grown." If only she realized how her decisions also affected me. It was a lot to process, so I slowly closed my eyes and hoped when I opened my eyes the next morning, I would be in Heaven. I needed God to save myself from this pit of hell.

Suddenly, I wake up super late that night—or maybe it's early morning. Either way, I know it's still dark outside, and I'm still loopy. The hospital discharges me and exports me to the psychiatric hospital. I had no idea what was ahead of me for the next week and a half. I check into the psych ward with my mother, and she has a bag of clothes for me. The first thing I noticed was that there were no windows. It looked like an asylum—all white, eerie, gloomy, and depressing; something you see in a movie. It felt as if my mind was walking into a cage. This wasn't a movie; this was real life. *I'm really here*, I instantly thought to myself. *Why in the heck am I here? This is going to make me crazy. There's no reason I should be here.*

I look at my mother and say, "Ma, I really don't need to be here."

"You don't have a choice," she responds.

"What about school and my classes?"

"I've made Dunwoody aware, and your teachers are aware."

Just great. Now, everyone is going to think I'm crazy.

We walk in and get me checked in. She's then told by a lady that she would take me from here, and visitation would be on Saturday during an allotted time slot. I would only be allowed to have an hour and a half with visitors, and only specified visitors would be allowed to come, which had to be listed on my paperwork. I then give my mom a hug and kiss and say goodbye. The nurse takes me down to the "kids' side" for girls. The hallway is super dark, and all the other patients are asleep. She advises me that the other side of the facility is for adults and points to that side. I'm told not to make any eye contact with the adult patients. I will have a specific time to wake up and eat. *You have to be kidding me*, I begin to think... While she's talking, I quickly remember, *Oh, shoot. It's that time of the month.*

"I'm on my cycle," I say to her.

"Okay, that's fine, but you can't have any tampons in your room. No bobby pins, rubber bands—nothing sharp. Oh, and you have to get your blood drawn each morning. Let me walk you to your room and show you where you'll put your toiletries. They have to be visible at all times. Panty liners are permissible."

As she's talking, I begin mentally drifting, as if the hallway is never ending. The doors look blurry, and everything around me feels surreal.

"I am not crazy!" I blurt out.

"I know you're not, but there's a reason why you felt the need to end your life, and we are going to work through what got you to this point."

Little did she know, there was no way I was going to confess to any of these people what got me to this point, and I surely wasn't going to speak about being molested.

I ended up being there for close to two weeks. During my counseling sessions, I said just enough to get them to believe I was okay. The funny thing is that the counselor, who was a male, told my mother I knew what to say just so I could get discharged. He wanted to break through my shell, but I wasn't having it. I

124

didn't trust men, so why would I open up to him? My time spent in the psychiatric hospital was the longest two weeks of my life. There was no access to or visuals of the outside world. The windows only allowed you to see across to the other side of the building.

In my opinion, it can drive someone to become and feel even crazier than who they are. It surely wasn't a place I needed to be admitted to as a teenager. What I really needed was deep therapy with a BLACK WOMAN. I needed to feel safe at home, to feel heard, and to feel understood. I needed to be saved, and I had no idea how to save myself. My mindset was processed as a victim. I mean, after all, I was a child with no tools or idea how to break free. I was a VICTIM, and lost, held hostage in my own mind and body.

The day I was discharged, it felt like freedom. I walked to my mother's car in silence. As she drove on the highway, I began looking around and taking it all in. I was literally stripped of my access to what I had been taking for granted. Watching the trees, the sun shining on my skin, just seeing the cars on the highways was beautiful. Those two weeks of being admitted changed my perception of things I had once taken for granted… freedom.

I vowed to myself to never end up back there, but the plot twist to that vow was followed by, "Girl, next time, you'd better follow through." See what I mean? I still wasn't healed—nowhere near it. I became a master at disguising all of my pain, but also at falling on my knees more often and praying to God. My prayers became conversations, and the only safe space I had, aside from talking to my Suga Mama. She was my prayer warrior. I prayed to God every night and asked for the strength to help me overcome my traumas.

God Is Stretching Me

As the oldest child, the weight of living up to a certain standard was a continuous burden. I placed such high expectations on myself, being my worst critic, despite graduating with honors from high school and my Alma Mater, Valdosta State University. Nothing was ever good enough for me. It felt as if I was a mouse on its spinning wheel, going in circle after circle. I wasn't fulfilled. Even after pledging Delta Sigma Theta Sorority, Inc., I still had this sense of incompleteness. I was pursuing all of my dreams—all while not addressing the deeper root of the pain and trauma I buried within.

From failed relationships to not understanding why I was so attached in those relationships, why did I so desperately want to be loved by a man while I didn't know how to love myself? Why was I searching for that forever man in high school and college? Why did I allow myself to be a fool in relationships? Why did I allow abuse to happen in my relationships? These were just a few areas I had to unpack in my twenties.

The journey in my twenties was rough. I was forced to face my reality. There was a plethora of anger and rage bottled up. Trusting people was nonexistent, especially with men. I expected the worst. My mentality was to never show what I was truly dealing with internally. Making myself vulnerable was a no-go; I couldn't risk allowing myself to seem weak. So, I continued to keep a strong exterior. But where did all of this stem from?

I didn't understand why until I truly began to heal, unpack, and face myself in my mid-twenties. This is when I truly had to relinquish control of myself and allow God to lead the way, all while I was also going to therapy. It was time to make a conscious decision to break through my trauma. I was tired of self-sabotaging relationships and having this "victim" mindset. I knew this was going to be a process. It was going to take time and intentionality on my end.

The first step was for me to finally be real with myself in that I was still hurt and carrying this load of trauma. I began going to church and following Bible plans within the Bible app. I would smudge my apartment with sage at least twice a week and would pray every day. A friend of mine introduced me to meditation and crystals. I kept myself on a consistent routine and learned how to love myself again. I didn't know how to receive love, and I realized it would begin with me understanding what it means to have self-love.

Although I was taking all these steps, there was a sense of unease in my then-role as an executive paralegal. Since the age of five years old, I had always dreamed of being an attorney. I used to joke about being better than Johnnie Cochran. I just knew becoming a nationally known attorney was my calling. My older cousin and Soror inspired me, as she was the only attorney in my family. I wanted to follow in her footsteps. So, in 2016, I took the LSAT twice, only to receive the exact same score both times, which is rare. I was head-down that entire year, so focused on getting into law school that I burnt myself taking the LSAT twice. That's actually something that is not recommended. Although I felt defeated and bummed by my score, I still applied to over twenty law schools with University of California (USC), University of California Los Angeles (UCLA), and Vanderbilt as my top three schools. My entire life was based around me being an attorney. I was even fortunate enough to receive a letter of recommendation by the County Attorney at the time.

After submitting all of my applications, the waiting game began. May and June passed, and all the while, I kept receiving denial letters, which sparked discouragement and caused depression and anxiety to resurface. By the end of July, I lost hope in receiving an offer letter, until one Thursday, I got mail from Howard University. My first thought was to throw it out. I was sick of receiving denial letters. However, God spoke to my spirit and said, "Open it." Initially, I was hesitant to do it, but I was obedient. Slowly opening the envelope, I pulled out the letter, and to my surprise, it read:

You have been accepted into Howard University School of Law.

In awe, I read the letter again. *Am I really reading this correctly? It's the end of July; why are they just now sending this to me? How will I pack up my whole apartment by next month? How am I supposed to move to DC in a month?* So many questions begin going through my mind, yet I am ecstatic.

I scream out, "Thank You, Lord!"

As tears are flowing, I dive deep into prayer. Everything seems to be falling into place. I'm working through my trauma, focused on healing and releasing, and now, I've been accepted into a law school. Although Howard wasn't in my top three, it was in my top ten schools. Later that weekend, I tell both my Suga Mama and mother about my acceptance letter. As any supportive mother and grandmother, they express their excitement and how proud they are of me. I was excited, too, but once the adrenaline died down, my spirit began feeling unsettled.

In the following week, while I'm working, I begin randomly seeing pop-ups about "timing." So, I go to an empty office and immediately pray, asking God if I should accept this letter: "I mean, why would You allow me to get into a law school, only to reveal to me that it's not time?" Well, that's exactly what He did. Although I received the acceptance letter thinking it was a sign, God was actually testing my faith to see if I would trust Him with the unknown. The timing wasn't conducive to me being able to move in such short notice. I had just renewed my lease, and God reminded me that He would not place anything in my life that would bring about confusion or chaos. But if it wasn't law school, then what else would I pursue? Although I didn't know what the future held, I chose not to accept the offer letter.

Towards the end of August, I was placed on FMLA due to my persistent and debilitating migraines and constant vertigo. It caused me to be unable to work for ten months. After choosing not to attend Howard University Law School, challenge after challenge continued to arise in my life. I had no idea after taking FMLA that it would be the beginning of my propulsion into a completely different career path. I never returned back to my position as an executive paralegal. In fact, God confirmed it was time for me to use my story to change lives, but not as an attorney. How could I use my story if I was still healing, though?

I didn't have all the answers, but I took out my retirement money, placed my resignation notice with the County Attorney's Office, and ended my journey in the legal industry. When I told my mother of my choice to pursue entrepreneurship, she was so upset I would be giving up on a career I talked about my entire life. She could not understand why. The only person who initially supported me was my Suga Mama, which meant the world to me, because I honestly did not even believe in myself. I had no idea where my life was headed. This was one of the most uncomfortable seasons of my life—no job, Ubering, and taking on contract roles, just trying to figure out what was next, all while I was healing from my childhood trauma. I cried so many nights. I was a single woman in the upscale Buckhead area in Georgia, in a beautiful apartment, yet with no clear direction.

Leap of Faith

God needed me to be in isolation in order for me to face my demons, truly work on myself, and ultimately hear His voice. He needed me to face everything head-on. No more running from the hurt. I worked out five times a week, and this was my therapeutic release.

Fitness became my outlet. I was always active, but during this season of my life, I began to tap into the mental and spiritual components of health and wellness. This is when I realized the transformative advantage the health and wellness industry possessed. As I've always had a passion for helping people, I began to think about who else was suffering. As I worked through my own traumas, it hit me that so many women are suffering in silence. I was overcoming my emotional, mental, and sexual abuse, and realizing health and wellness can transform others' lives just as it was transforming mine. As the determined and ambitious woman I always was, I decided to study for my personal trainer certification. I passed on the first try and obtained my certification through ISSA (International Sports Sciences Association). Then, life hit me again. We found out my grandmother's ovarian cancer had returned, and this time around, it was more aggressive. I was so heartbroken; I couldn't fathom life without her. I began diving deeper into prayer for God's healing to enter her body.

During one of my weekly calls with my Suga Mama, I shared the news with her that I passed my certification. After she congratulated me, I began stuttering. I was so nervous, but I went for it.

"Suga Mama, I want to ask you something. What do you think about me starting my own health and wellness business as a fitness and wellness professional?"

She immediately responded and said she would support me one hundred percent, and I would be an amazing business owner. Her words were enough confirmation for me. It was exactly what I needed to hear.

"Do you have a name yet?" she asked.

"No, not yet. That's the next goal, and to register it as an LLC."

I went to the drawing board and began thinking of business names. It didn't take me long to land on "Warrior Queen B F.I.T.," and my tribe of clientele would be known as the "Warrior Queen Tribe." Everything I had been through in my life that was meant to defeat me were bricks helping me build my foundation. Warrior Queen was derived from my story and the story of the strength I witnessed from my grandmother. She was the strongest woman I knew. Every tear, every cut, every suicidal thought, being molested, enduring emotional abuse, failed relationships, attempting to end my own life, was all meant to land me exactly where I was supposed to be—to be a testament to other women and girls who are suffering that they, too, can overcome. Depression and anxiety do not have to control us.

And most importantly, I am no longer a victim. I am a SURVIVOR. I am a WARRIOR QUEEN! And so are you! We can thrive!

My faith in God kept me going even when I couldn't find a way out. I easily could have died in that hospital room when I popped all those pills, but God had a greater purpose for me. I didn't understand what it was until I began trusting Him, surrendering it all to Him, and focusing on my own healing. This is my story, and I took control of the narrative. I had to take control of my future, and I made the decision to stop allowing my past to define my present. I realized that I had the power to change how I saw myself and that my life is defined by what God called me to be, not by my transgressions.

Despite what life brings your way, there's always light at the end of the tunnel. I know that sounds cliche; however, it's true. We are meant to GROW through what we GO through. It took me years of keeping the faith and taking life one step at a time. I had to learn how to receive love and forgive my stepfather for the abuse he inflicted onto me. I had to learn how to forgive those who hurt me—not for them, but for ME and my own healing. I had to forgive myself for not knowing how to love me properly. I had to fight through the disappointments and the feelings of abandonment and discouragement. So many nights felt like hell, but my faith kept me afloat. What if I had given up? I wouldn't be able to share my story as I am now.

God never left my side, just as He hasn't left yours. I saved the little girl within, and I'm still on this constant quest of healing. My trauma will always be with me, but it is no longer controlling me. It took me years to learn how to identify my triggers, how to set boundaries, and how to trust God with my life through faith, deep prayer, and self-healing. Every day may not bring sunshine, but I take each day as a new opportunity to be better than the last. I thank God for never leaving my side.

I live out my life through my own personal mantra, and I suggest you do the same, too: "Fight from the inside out."

"A Warrior Queen is a woman who keeps her crown held high, takes the stones that were thrown at her, and uses them as strength to help build the foundation of her life. She allows herself to feel her emotions, never running from her truth, yet she faces everything head-on and seeks not to be viewed as a victim, but as a survivor on a constant journey to thrive and shine. She straightens her crown when it tilts and gives herself the love she knows she deserves .

With each challenge, she grows mentally and spiritually, RELENTLESSLY working every day towards becoming her best self and healing from the inside out. She understands her quest to heal, and

through her faith in God, it is a decision she must make on a daily basis. She trusts that everything will work out for her greater good."

— Queen Bohannon

Proverbs 31:25 — "She is clothed with strength and dignity, and she laughs without fear of the future."

Queen Bohannon

Chapter 7

Young, Uneducated, and Impregnated

I was born to the amazing parents, Frank and Betty Williams, on August 6, 1961. My upbringing was probably typical, like that of most children in America. But unlike most of the families in my neighborhood, my parents were married and loving, and they took good care of us. I am the sixth child and the first girl. Yes, I had five older brothers who loved me very much, and each was uniquely different from the other. My older two brothers lived with my mother's oldest sister, Rosa Lee Waterman. We affectionately called her Cap—short for Captain. She never had any children. She asked my mother if they could live with her, and my mother agreed. My mother would later regret that decision.

She believed that she should have reared her own children. My oldest brother, Gregory A. Lewis, was six years older than me. He was kind, loving, always smiling with those beautiful dimples and those pearly white teeth, easygoing, handsome, and a smart young man. He enjoyed playing basketball with his friends. Every now and then, I would watch them play, running up and down the court, pushing, and talking trash to one another. Although I didn't understand the game that much, I was proud of my brother because other children would talk about how great he was. They would say things like, "Wow! He should be playing with the pros! He's incredible," and I would agree. It was streetball, but we enjoyed watching the raw talent that those young guys had. He always dressed to impress. He would wear his Polo-style T-shirt, with pressed khaki pants and his clean Converse sneakers.

Brother number two is Gary Lewis; he was a year behind Greg. Gary loved music. He knew all the latest dances; it's only befitting that he played in his high school band. He served in the Army for five years. He loved cracking jokes on his friends and family. My third brother, Trenton E. Lewis, was always in charge of the younger siblings. He was thinner than my older brothers; he was truly skinny and frail. He did not participate in any of the sports or arts. He was the bookworm, the educator. Even at a young age, he had excellent study habits; he won many oratorical contests, he would study the Bible, he checked and helped us with our homework, and he was always teaching us about God.

Our mother trained us to listen and to respect our older siblings. If one of us got out of line when she was not at home, the older brother could correct the behavior. He had a desk with a chair that he used when we were being homeschooled, way before homeschooling was popular. He was invested in our learning, and he wanted us to excel. When we need help, we would go to him, our in-house tutor/teacher. It's no surprise to us that he would be the first to go to college. He graduated from The University of Florida and later received his master's degree from Harvard. He also spent twenty years in the Army, reaching the ranks as Lieutenant Colonel.

My fourth brother, Shawn Williams, was affectionately called "White Boy or Whitey." He loved sports; he played high school football, and he was also on the track team. He was pretty good at both. Living in the housing projects, physical fights were an everyday occurrence. Shawn would stand up for those who were being bullied. He would say to our schoolmates, "Pick on someone who will fight back. Picking on someone you know can beat is crazy." He didn't go looking for fights, but he would not back down from one, either. He was very competitive. I remember on one occasion, one of the neighborhood boys in the community was feared by most of the boys his age. He was a good fighter, and we were afraid of him. I'm not sure what happened, but the word got out in the hood that he wanted to fight Shawn. I must admit that Shawn had a mean streak, and he was ready. Well, you probably guessed it: Shawn beat the bully down, and we didn't have any more issues with him. He came to respect him. Shawn was the second brother to join the military, and he served in the Army for twenty years.

My fifth brother, Vander, had a beautiful chocolate completion; his skin was even-toned and flawless. I can't recall him ever having acne. Some of the family members would affectionately call him "Shine." He was a year older than me. He was quiet and easy going, he enjoyed family and friends, and he was a Mama's Boy. He liked Shawn, he loved football, and he was also on the track team. After high school graduation, he also joined the Army, where he served in the military for four years. As you can tell, we were stairstep children.

Then, here comes me. My mother prayed for years for me; she asked God to bless her with a girl child. I can only imagine that with every birth, she was hoping and praying that the baby would be a girl. I am sure that each time she became pregnant, she would ask God for three things: Let the baby be born healthy, let the baby be a girl, and allow her to live until all her children were grown. And I believe that she experienced several different emotions after the first son. She was likely excited that she had a healthy baby, and probably a little disappointed that she had not yet received the female child that she so desired.

She would tell me time and time again how she had asked God to bless her with me; she had promised Him that she would take special care of me. She told Him that she would make all my clothes, and that she would breastfeed me. On that faithful Sunday morning, August 6, 1961, God honored her request after many years of praying for me. I was born. I can only imagine her sheer delight; she had to be shedding tears of joy, overwhelmed with gratitude while she prayed and praised God. I am sure it was love at first sight. A dream delayed was not a dream denied. Mother tried to breastfeed me, but she stated that I would not latch on, and she didn't have anyone to assist her as she tried to navigate this new process. It's also possible that I was experiencing nipple confusion. Whatever it was, she did not breastfeed me or any of my siblings.

Four years later, she had my sister, Tanakia, also known as Lynn Williams. She was beautiful and outgoing. She had many friends; she was the social butterfly. She got into many fights when she was young. She was no pushover. She was outspoken and a cheerleader. She studied cosmetology at Tampa Bay Tech Vocational High School, and she and her model friend, Wanda Barkley, won the statewide hair competition.

She was also her class's best-dressed female. After graduation, she married, became a military wife, and was able to travel the world. She later decided to go to Fayetteville State University, where she received her Bachelor of Science degree, and she later received her master's degree from Troy State University. Three years later, mother had the sixth boy, the eighth child, Frank L. Williams; we affectionately call him Lil Frank.

Baby brother has also been very loving and easygoing. He did not participate in any sports. He was also very studious; he loved math. I truly believe that he could solve any math problem that he faced. He once sent a math equation to a company with the hope that it would be patented, and after many months, he received a letter indicating that the equation was already discovered. We did not believe them because he had researched the information before submitting his work. He enjoyed spinning music; he was the family DJ.

He graduated from The University of South Florida. A year later, Mother had our sister, Vandella Nicole Williams. She was the ninth child and the third girl. Nicole was fun-loving; we would tease her and state that, being that she was born June 19 under the zodiac sign of Gemini, her twin, Gertrude, would come out when she was upset. She was such a family girl. She was a dancerette in high school, she had many friends, and she would style my hair better than any hairstylist that I have ever used. She loved fashion—a true fashionista. After graduating from Tampa Bay Tech Vocational High School, she and her boyfriend, L.C. Johnson, Sr., welcomed their first born beautiful baby girl, LaDreauna C. Johnson. She later received her Associate of Arts Degree from Hillsborough Community College. Six years later, Mother had her tenth and final child at the mature age of forty years old: her fourth girl, our baby sister, Treemonisha S. Williams. We affectionately call her Tree. She was quiet, very reserved, fun-loving, and like most babies, a little spoiled.

You see, our mother never wanted any children. She was raised by her oldest sister, Rosa Lee Waterman, after their mother died when she was about five years old. Mother had a chocolate complexion. She was five feet, three inches tall, with a medium frame. She had the Stoney family's signature trait, diastema (gap teeth). She was a curvy woman with beautiful legs, like that of a dancer. She was the disciplinarian of the family. We respected her like our lives depended on it. Although all my brothers towered over her, they never challenged her; they were respectful and well-mannered. Mother did not play. When she asked us to do a task, we knew that she meant for us to do it right then. Not in a minute or when we felt like it, but right then, without delay.

My mom maintained a clean house and yard; she believed that cleanliness was next to godliness. We were not allowed to get up at any hour of the day on the weekends. We could sleep in usually as late as 8:00 a.m. If she didn't have chores that required immediate attention. She was also an excellent cook, and she could sew and make different outfits for us. She was a wonderful caregiver when we were sick, which didn't happen often. She would nurse us back to health, sometimes with home remedies. Our Aunt Cap would give each of us a dose of cod liver oil every Saturday morning; she would say that we needed a good cleaning out. The downfall to that weekly regimen was that we only had one bathroom, but we managed just fine.

One of my favorite hobbies growing up was riding my bike. I didn't learn to ride until I was about nine years old. But once I learned to ride, I would ride up and down on my street, in front of my house that was located at 1257 Joed Court in Tampa, Florida. It was a low-income housing project. I must admit that I didn't know we were poor. Everyone in the neighborhood had just about the same things, often with no car, extra money, or resources. I had three pairs of shoes. You guessed it: a pair for church, a pair for school, and a pair for play. When I wanted to go outside to play or for a ride, I had to change into play clothes and shoes!

Most of the families in our community would receive food stamps to help feed their children, and the working parents often were earning minimum wages. Sometimes, they earned enough to pay rent and utilities. Thank God for Medicaid that took care of our medical needs. Our mothers would line up once a month to receive the supply of government food. The food supply consisted of a block of cheese, can of SPAM, sugar, butter, powdered milk, and flour. The American cheese was great for making grilled cheese sandwiches, and my mother's macaroni and cheese was second to none; it was simply amazing.

She taught me how to prepare it for the family. I loved learning how to cook with her. She cooked with love and soul. One day I went for a ride, and a car was coming. I didn't see the car. The middle-aged white man, dressed in a gray suit with a white shirt, hit me hard enough to throw me from the bike and onto the ground. He stopped suddenly, parked his car, and ran from his car towards me to come see if I was okay. Thank GOD, I was. I can't say the same about the bike. The rear tire was bent, and I was unable to ride it.

He asked if I was okay. I quickly replied yes. I wanted him to leave me alone so that I could collect myself and cry, trying to fight back the tears. I was embarrassed and afraid that I would be in trouble once I got home. The bike accident was not my fault, and I wasn't sure how I was going to tell my mother; I just knew my mother would be upset with me. The bike was a Christmas gift, and now, it was broken. Money was limited, or sometimes, we had none at all.

Unfortunately for me, the man who hit me insisted that he take me home and inform my mother about the accident and to explain to her what happened. He followed me while I tried to push a bike that didn't work properly. Once I arrived home, a block away from where the incident took place, all I could think of was what my punishment would be. As we reached the front of the house, it appeared that my mom had been awaiting my arrival.

The businessman spoke up and said, "Hello, ma'am. My name is Mike H., and I didn't see your daughter riding her bike. I accidentally hit her. She said that she was fine. If you would, take her to the doctor for me to be sure she is. I will pay the bill. And if you don't mind, I would like to take the bike to the repair shop and return it once it's fixed.

He appeared to be more nervous than I was. I was relieved that she didn't yell at me, or worse—spank me! Mr. Mike H. gave my mother his business card. She gave me a hug once she realized that I was okay. My parents took me to the doctor's office the next day, and everything was fine. The following week or so. Mr. Mike H. returned my bike, and I was thrilled! It looked brand new; it was pink with a white flower basket attached.

"Thank you, Mr. Mike!" I said with excitement.

My prized possession was finally home again. I was very careful after that accident—no more automobile crashes. That was the year I met my best friend, Teresa Brewer; we were in the same sixth grade class at Meacham Elementary School. Our teacher was Mr. Moses. We talked to each other after school almost every day. We had a lot in common; she was the middle child, and like me, she was the first girl. She had two older brothers, a younger sister and a younger brother. Her mother was a beautiful, short, petite woman; she was very friendly, always smiling, and soft-spoken. She was married to George Williams. Her name was Betty Williams, just like my mother. By the time we got to junior high school, our friendship continued to flourish. On occasion, I was able to visit her home. Her family lived just a few blocks from us.

During one of my many visits, I met her older brother, Ronald. He was sixteen years old, with a dark chocolate complexion, a slender medium frame, and slight bowlegs. He stood at about five feet, nine inches, with the most radiant, beautiful smile. His teeth were perfectly even, with no gaps or protruding teeth. He was a junior in high school when I met him. He was truly handsome. I spoke to him in passing, and shortly thereafter, I returned home.

The next day in school, Teresa told me that her brother asked about me and that he wanted to talk to me. I started to smile, thinking that he wasn't really interested in me. He was older, and with his good looks, he could probably have any girl in our neighborhood or at his school. I was not allowed to talk to boys until I was sixteen, so Teresa would call and give him the phone so my parents wouldn't know that I was talking on the phone with a boy. But Ronald was not just any boy; we were moving towards him becoming my boyfriend. We started talking on the phone more and more, and I was falling in LOVE with him.

We only had one phone line; therefore, our telephone conversations were short and sweet. We talked about school, family, friends, what our future plans were, hobbies, our relationship, his love for basketball, and being in love. In my mind, we were becoming good friends—or, shall I say ,boyfriend and girlfriend. I enjoyed getting to know him over the phone. I was so excited when he would call me.

Our first kiss would not just be a peck on the lips, but a real wet kiss. He told me that we were going to be tonguing, French kissing. I had no idea what that meant or how to do it, but my boyfriend was going to teach me. He told me what to expect, that I needed to close my eyes and trust him. It was a wet kiss. I was nervous, but as time went on, he would continue to encourage me to relax, which was very difficult to do. Over time, I was getting the hang of it, but he would tell me that I would jump as if I was still a little nervous. The relationship between us continued to evolve; he started talking about sex and making love. I reminded him that I was a virgin and was not ready for making love or having sex. I thought to myself, *After all, I am only thirteen years young.* I wondered if other thirteen-year-old girls were having sex:

Were they in love? What was it like? Did they enjoy it? I assured myself that there was no way I was ready for that next step. My parents would kill me. My dad was a preacher, and my mother was strict. *Oh, NO! Not me,* I thought. Our relationship was growing stronger and stronger. He was sixteen years old and had experienced sex before, and he wanted me to experience, it too. He stated that he would take good care of me, that he loved me. After about several months of saying no and that I was not ready for sex, I was so nervous as we kissed, and he was touching my body in places that were private. He started to undress himself and then me. I said we had to stop. He stopped and began to re-assure me that everything would be okay. He kissed me again. He told me that if I loved him, I could do it. My hands began to sweat, as they always do when I am experiencing mixed emotions and a sense of nervousness.

142

He took off my clothes, and I would not allow him to take off my bra or panties. I felt my shorts fall down around my ankles. I started to grow more anxious. What am I doing here? What is going to happen next? My mother will kill me. He pulled the covers back as I stood there with my bra and panties on. I was afraid, but I felt that this was the only way I had to prove my undying love for him. As he took my hand and assisted me to get in the bed, my heart was racing. I could hear each beat, and they were getting louder and louder as he continued kissing me. He then climbed on top of me while opening my legs that were pressed tightly together, and I could not relax myself. Afraid, anxious, scared, nervous, naïve, and in love—that's a dangerous situation.

The penetration was unbearable.

"You must stop!" I cried out. "It hurts too much."

Once again, he tried to reassure me that because it was my first time, it would hurt only this one time. He was lightyears ahead of me, and he pulled out the Vaseline.

I asked, "What's that for, and where did it come from?"

He told me it would help me. He attempted to penetrate me again after applying the Vaseline. The pain was more intense. I began to cry.

"You're hurting me! You must stop right now!"

He tried to soothe me yet again, but this time, it didn't work. It was finally over. The sheets where we laid were soiled with blood, semen, and Vaseline. He got up and went to the restroom. I could hear the water running. He came back with a washcloth. He asked If I was okay. I said NO—NOT AT ALL! My vaginal area was hurting so badly. I tried to collect myself as he was smiling, asking me again and again if I was okay. How could I be okay, behaving like a full-grown woman? I felt horrible and ashamed; I was disappointed in myself. I tried to get up and go to the bathroom. I could barely walk; every step I took was painful. Then, he said my mother would be home soon, and we needed to go. My hair was disheveled. I could barely walk. He kissed me again and told me how much he loved me, and now, he knew how much I loved him. He started calling me more on the phone.

I could not date yet; my parents had told me I was too young. Wow…

"But I'm thirteen!" I exclaimed. My mom insisted that I had to be sixteen.

We would have to keep our love a secret, but not for long. I had started my period about six months prior. It was now November 1974, and my cycle had not come for that month. I panicked. *Oh, no! Why is my period late?* I thought to myself. Although I had only had my menstrual cycle for a few months, it was never late. *Oh, my God. I can't be pregnant, not after one encounter*, I thought as I was waiting for my menstrual cycle to start. Although I had no cramps, I was looking for any sign that it was about to start. I called my girlfriend, and she reassured me that I was not pregnant, not after that one time. Now, please note that she had never been pregnant, and she was just shy of fifteen years old herself. But I believed her. However, days turned into weeks, and weeks turned into months.

I told my boyfriend what was going on and that my cycle still had not come. I expressed how bad this would be for me— my mother would literally kill me if she found out that I had sex, and secondly, if I was, in fact, pregnant! She was the disciplinary parent—not my dad. I couldn't recall a time when my father had chastised me, but my mother put the fear of GOD in me—in all my siblings, for that matter.

That gave him an idea that might work to help me lose the baby: "If you can get wasted on alcohol, that would cause you to have a miscarriage." The main problem with that idea was that I didn't drink. I had never had a taste of any alcoholic drink before. Then, I came up with an idea of maybe getting hit by a car. I figured I would be banged up, but that it would help me lose the baby. Ultimately, neither of us had a solution. He told me he was going to tell his mother, and she could tell my mother. I begged him not to do that. My mother made it clear that she never wanted to learn anything about her children from anyone in the street. We needed to tell her before someone else outside of the family did.

One day, I overheard my mother telling her sisters, my aunts, that she dreamed of fish! My heart sank when I heard that. In our family, we believe that God sends messages through dreams. A fish dream meant that someone was or would be pregnant soon.

As weeks went on, I would put on my sanitary napkin to pretend that my period was on, with no period still. I would hold my stomach in whenever I was at home. Then, one day after school, she looked at me and said, "Sassy, you are pregnant." Her eyes were filled with tears.

I shook my head and said, "No, ma'am."

I wanted to confirm that her suspicion was right, but I was too scared. I felt so bad. She was the one person who truly loved me unconditionally, and I had hurt her so much. *What's next? Is she going to put me out? If so, where will I go? I don't want to live without my family.* I was too young to be having sex, and yet, much too young to be pregnant. A million questions ran through my head. *God, please help me. I don't know what to do. I don't know where to go. How can I handle all this pressure?* I brought shame to myself and my family. I hated seeing my family trying to process the here and now and what my future would be like. I felt so alone, sad, and confused. I can only imagine that my mother must have cried to my dad many nights, and they both endured sleepless nights.

The next day or so, I was at the doctor's office, and yes, he confirmed my greatest fear. I was about eight weeks pregnant. He told my parents to schedule my prenatal appointment. He never mentioned anything about other alternatives. One painful sexual encounter created all this turmoil.

My mother informed Ronald's parents, and they were supportive. I didn't want to receive prenatal care from the health department because I didn't want everyone to know about the pregnancy. I didn't want to be judged by my peers and my community. Who was I kidding? This was the housing project, and once the word got out to one person, I could write it off. Secrets and protecting one's privacy were nonexistent.

After everyone digested the news, I asked my mother if we could continue my prenatal care with Dr. Donahue, and to my surprise, she said yes. I could not stop apologizing to my mother and father for the hurt, shame, and disappointment that I created. It was almost unbearable for me to see the pain in my mother's eyes, and she could see pain in mine. She never ordered me out of the house. She told me it was my baby, not hers or my dad's, and I now had to be responsible and accountable for my actions. Remember, in the beginning, I told you how much my mother prayed for a girl and about her promise to God that if He blessed her, she would take great care of me. She honored her word to God.

I'm sure she had no idea that she would be tested like this. The one thing that I knew for sure was that my parents loved me, especially my mother. I was in the ninth grade, and I was pregnant. The pregnancy went well. I never experienced morning sickness or any other illness. Unfortunately, I was riddled with guilt and shame. Everyone had something to say—classmates, schoolmates, teachers, church members, and strangers. Everywhere I went, people talked about me. I began to keep myself from the cruel world. My neighbors talked about me every time they saw me. I can remember hearing them saying things like, "After all, she's just a baby herself. What is she going to do with a baby? "It's a shame. She's fast." Fast was another term for "loose" or "out of control." Truth be told, I was none of those things. I felt so alone.

You see, being a teen mom during those days was not the norm. I was ostracized, the black sheep of the neighborhood. Did I mention that my dad was a preacher and I still had to attend church? Several months after I got pregnant, we moved in June of 1975. The home was huge. It was a Victorian-style four-bedroom home, with two-and-a-half baths, a laundry room, a beautiful front porch, a Florida room, commonly known as a den, and a shed that would double as a fifth bedroom. We were moving on UP! Just like the Jeffersons! I was uneducated, pregnant, and filled with shame and embarrassment for my family and loved ones. I didn't know what to expect next.

I prayed that GOD would bless me, my baby, and my family. I knew that one day, I would make my parents proud of me. I was probably harder on myself than any of my brothers and sisters. They continued to love me no matter what. They were never disrespectful to me; they truly loved me, despite my circumstance. I didn't want to leave the safety of my village. I was going to be the best mother that I could be. After all, I had an amazing, beautiful, praying role model: my mother. I didn't have a baby shower; no one wanted to celebrate the new arrival for a young girl who was pregnant out of wedlock. I realized that this new life growing inside of me needed all my love and affection. I prayed daily that one day, GOD would see me through the hurt, pain, and shame. He did; He never left my side. I continued with school and church. I needed both. I had hopes and dreams. I wanted more out of life than to be a teen mom.

One morning, at around 1:00 a.m., I was awakened by painful contractions. I knew that it was about time for the baby. I ate healthy meals throughout the pregnancy, and I walked through the community park with my little sisters regularly. I knew I had to do right by this baby; we would grow up together. I maintained all my prenatal care appointments. I had prepared my bag for the hospital. I had a few gowns, along with a robe, a bra, panties, a toothbrush, toothpaste, house shoes, and a baby blanket. My mother made sure that I had everything that I would need for my hospital stay. My overnight bag was ready.

On August 3, 1975, three days shy of my fourteenth birthday, it was time for the baby. The contractions were getting stronger and stronger. When I could no longer withstand the pain, I went to my mother. She got up, and we started timing the contractions; they were coming every ten minutes. As the early morning grew, so did the pain. My parents took me to Tampa General Hospital, and I was admitted. The pain was becoming more intense. I couldn't accurately describe it; I just knew it was something I had never experienced. Thank GOD for pain medicine. My mother stayed by my side throughout the entire process. I know it had to be one of the hardest things to witness, watching your own child in such pain. As the pain intensified, my mother would call the nurse to come to my aid. She prayed for me. I can still hear her wringing her hands, asking GOD to take care of me from the time I got to the hospital until I delivered. I kept thinking back to that one sexual encounter, and now, I was in active labor, having my own baby. Wow! Talk about disbelief!

We now had a beautiful baby girl, weighing seven pounds and seven ounces. I had a vaginal delivery, and my bottom was quite sore. This labor and delivery process was very intense and serious; nothing could prepare me for what had just transpired. Childbirth was no joke. It was a very serious and life-changing event. After the delivery, my baby and I were doing fine. I had my six weeks postpartum appointment with Dr. Donohue. He talked with me and mother about birth control pills, and he gave me different pamphlets and books.

I was so young and inexperienced with this new role as mom. My baby girl was so beautiful. We named her Renelia Lazora Brewer. According to my mother, she was a typical baby. She was a happy, healthy baby. Of course the crying, sleepless nights, and teething were all challenging, especially for a teen mom who was a student in school. She was bottle fed; no one discussed breastfeeding options.

Ronald's visits and telephone calls were becoming less and less frequent. I had heard rumors that he was seeing another girl. I asked him about the rumors, and of course, he denied them. I was now a sophomore at Robinson High School and a teenage mom. Ronald was now a senior at the same high school, but we had double sessions. The juniors and seniors began school an hour or so earlier than the sophomores, so I didn't get a chance to see him much. Our relationship was growing tense. He didn't come around as often. He had it going on with the girls, but we were supposed to stay together forever. Well, forever was short-lived. I wanted to make our relationship work. So, one night, he came by to see me and our baby, who we affectionately called Renee. She was now three months old. My mother was asleep, and he wanted to have sex with me—or "make love," as he would call it.

I said, "I can't. My mother is sleeping, and if we got caught, that would be the end of me."

This young boy had such control over me. I gave in. I reminded him that I wasn't on birth control yet and that he needed to wait, but his needs were greater than my logic. By now, this was probably our fifth or sixth sexual encounter, and our second time having sex since we had our daughter. My mother got up from her bed because of the noise she heard. She walked into the room just as Ronald was pulling up his pants. She was so livid. Here we were with a three-month-old baby girl, and once again, I had found myself in an uncontrollable and unnecessary position.

She has done so much for me and Renee. Why didn't I insist that he wait? I don't know if it's because I thought he loved me, or because I was peer pressured. Or, was I too scared to tell him no? I was afraid that I would lose him. I am sure it was a combination of all four. Perhaps, I valued his needs over mine.

Once again, a month later, no period.

"Oh, GOD, this can't be happening to me again!" I cried out to the Lord.

I even tried to bargain with GOD, but that didn't help. Who gets pregnant a second time after everything I had been through? Silly me! *Is this real?* The first time, my family accepted what I had done. I'm sure they didn't expect to have to embrace yet another baby. They said I made a mistake the first time, but now, what would they say about this time? I questioned myself, searching for answers.

I couldn't tell them again. What would, or could, I even say? Once again, I said nothing, and again, the fish dream was mentioned. I had absolutely no doubt that my mother would surely put us out this time. *Where will I go?* I begin to cry and pray.

"Lord, please forgive me for my sins. Please don't leave me," I prayed unto my Lord.

I was only 14 years old, and now, I was pregnant again for the second time. I thought about the dumb decision I had made.

I became very frustrated with myself and with Ronald. I regretted giving in to Ronald; I had been more concerned with his needs than my own. Why wasn't I on birth control pills? Dr. Donohue stated that after having Renee, there was an increased chance of getting pregnant again if I didn't use a contraceptive. He was right!

I told Ronald about the pregnancy, and he asked me one of the most profound questions I had ever heard: "Who is the father?" Wow! Are you kidding me? I was totally caught off guard. Was this a joke? Was he accusing me of being unfaithful? Was he serious? Was this another way to say that he wanted out? Although we had only a few sexual encounters, I was pregnant a second time. I was heartbroken when I realized that he was serious. I couldn't sleep at night; I wasn't eating much, either. I had no one else to confide in. Once again, I was pregnant and alone. I asked God to give me the strength to make it through this teen mom process and not to let me give up on myself.

Our relationship was over! I didn't have but a few maternity clothes, so I had to wash them constantly, and they were wearing thin. I remember standing on the courtyard at Robinson High School, and one of my classmates noticed a small hole in my top. She had to take the liberty to point it out before me and what felt like the entire student body. She was loud and proud to embarrass me.

Immediately, another classmate said with a loud voice, "So what? Leave Cannella alone. Y'all always trying to start some mess."

I never had any more issues with her or anyone else at school. It felt good knowing that one person wanted to befriend me, and a new friendship evolved with my new best friend, Gaynell Johnson. She was one of the few classmates who would talk to me, and she wasn't ashamed to be seen with me. Our friendship grew rapidly. She was skinny, with a smooth, chocolate-brown complexion. She was very vocal and outspoken; she would tell you off if you got things twisted. She was a true friend. We never argued or belittled one another; we never fought or cursed each other out. She would always encourage me, as I would her.

Her family was like my extended family. She was from a large family; her mother had eleven children. She was the baby girl of the family, and she was a fraternal twin. (She had a twin brother.) She has been a part of my life and my family for over forty-five years. She would come over to my house, and we would talk for hours about everything—her male friend, her love life, school, church, our families, our friends. She'd ask me how I was handling the pregnancy. She would help me with my chores by washing dishes, hanging up clothes on the clothesline, folding clothes, and cooking with me and my mother. She would help me with Renee.

We would walk to the park with Renee. It was so beautiful; it had a pond with so many different ducks and birds, benches, a playground, a pavilion for picnics or parties, a football and baseball field, a basketball court, and tennis courts. Everything was so well maintained. We also had a recreation center. Wow! This was the good life. It was very different from Central Park Housing Projects, where our park was always in need of repairs. Most of the birds that we saw were pigeons. I loved my new community, and I love my BFF so very much! She was beautiful, inside and out.

Ronald, on the other hand, had awakened a strong young Black girl consciousness. I did not know my strength or my power, but I continued to pray, trust God, and believe that things would get better for me. I had to move forward. I could not give up. I was not going to stop. As a matter of fact, Ronald and I never had sex again after that night, but that didn't change the fact that I was pregnant. His parents, once again, came through for us. The two Bettys were awesome, amazing, wonderful, loving, supportive women for me and my girls. I truly believed that they did not want either of us to fail as parents, in school, or in life. We had moved out of the projects, so I no longer had to hear the negative comments from the women in my old community. No one knew me.

I felt free from my old environment and from Ronald. On August 1, 1976, I had my second adorable daughter, Vandora Romekia Brewer. People thought that she was mixed with Asian or something because of her very beautiful slanted eyes. She and Renee were referred to as Irish twins because they were less than one year apart. My labor and delivery process was very intense, and my favorite girl was, once again, by my side. I know, without a shadow of a doubt, that my mother truly loved me. She never gave up on me; she was always there for me and my girls. I could never repay her or my father for all that they did and endured. 1 Peter 4:8 always comes to mind when I think about all that transpired: "And above all things, have fervent love for one another, for love will cover a multitude of sins."

I thanked God for another vaginal delivery, and another perfect girl. She weighed in at seven pounds even, and once again, we bottle fed her. After we relocated, I transferred to Hillsborough High School for my junior and senior years. It was a new beginning for me and my family. I loved the school right away. It was huge, with three floors and stained glass windows. It was one of the oldest schools in Florida. The red brick school was warm and exciting. My classmates didn't know my history; they barely knew my name, and that was fine with me. I could be a student without all the judgment. I understand why people move away from a community, city, or state and never look back.

I felt freedom like never before, with a new home and a new school. Thank you, Jesus, for all the many blessings that you have given us. I could choose who I wanted to share my story with. I felt, for the first time in my life, that I was in control. I met a classmate, and I was the new girl on campus, all of 105 pounds. His name was Rob Jenkins, and he told me about this wonderful program for students that wanted to go to college, called Upward Bound. He asked if I had plans to go to college. I was taken aback and said, "Oh, yes!" He told me to go and see our guidance counselor, Ms. Hilton.

She was a beautiful, young Black lady; she didn't look much older than the students. I asked for the Upward Bound application, and she gave it to me with a warm smile. Then, she told me that I needed to return it to her right away because the last day to turn them in was quickly approaching. Many years later, I learned that she was a Florida Agricultural and Mechanical

University graduate. I held the application close to me. I took it home and told my mother about this wonderful opportunity and that I needed to call my older brother, Trenton. He was a student at The University of Florida. I had to ask permission to make a long-distance call, and my mother agreed that I could call him. The application required my parents' income information, and I knew that was going to be a problem. They protected their financial earnings. Once I had him on the telephone, I began to share with him the program requirements. He was knowledgeable about the program, and he asked me to mail it to him.

My brother had prepared financial documents for our parents in the past, but this matter was too important to me to mail. I insisted that he come home for the weekend because of the time constraints. With a little begging and pleading, he agreed to come home. I stayed at his side while he read and completed the forms. I found the ink pen. I got him something to eat, and when he finished, I was so excited. He was my hero; my big brother took care of everything. The next week, I returned all the documents, and now, I had to wait and see if I was approved for the program. A short time later, I received my letter in the mail. I was accepted into the Upward Bound Program.

The program was just what I needed; it changed the trajectory of my life. I had never heard about this program, and it was one of the greatest decisions that my parents could have made for me. The first weekend that we met was for orientation, and we had to adhere to the rules. Our program took place at The University of South Florida. There were students from the neighboring Polk, Manatee, and Pasco counties; it wasn't just for the students in Hillsborough County. It was amazing. We received a stipend, and we had the liberty to eat in the cafeteria. The cafeteria had so many food options: hot plates, cold plates, soups, a salad bar, sandwich stations, desserts, and drink fountains. I had never seen so many food options or choices in my life at a university or college. I was overjoyed to be a part of this program. Mr. Richard F. Pride was the director of the Upward Program. I have no idea of the number of children's lives that he impacted—my guess is that there were hundreds or thousands of us.

Unfortunately, Rob did not fare well with the program. He violated one of the rules and was dismissed from the program. While attending Hillsborough High School, I met another very good friend, Roberta Smith. She and I had something in common: She was also a teen mom. We became close friends, and she was just a delight. She was full of laughter. She would tell us about her family and friends, and she would have us dying laughing. On occasion, she would wear her big Afro. Her family was exceptionally kind; her mother and older brother were a lot of fun. She was a smart girl; we had the same English class. One day, we were in the cafeteria, and I saw Anthony Mutcherson.

I asked her, "Who is that?"

She replied, "Oh, that ain't no one but Anthony."

I said to her, "He is handsome."

She asked if I wanted to meet him, and I said YES with such excitement. She beckoned for him to come over, and he did, and she made the introductions. He was light brown and about five feet, eight inches tall. His smile was radiant; his teeth were beautiful. He was easy on the eyes. He asked me if he could walk me to my class, and I said yes. He took my books, walked me to class, and kissed me on the forehead. The young man was smooth. When class ended, he was at the door, waiting for me to exit. I was in shock; we both began to smile from ear to ear. He was a perfect gentleman. We exchanged telephone numbers, and from that day forth, he would walk me to class. We would talk on the phone for hours, talking each other to sleep. We never wanted to hang up the phone. I could not wait for the next day of school; I wanted to see him more and more. I told him about my girls, and of course, he didn't believe me. So, he came over to my house to see them for himself. He thought, like most people, that they were my little sisters. I assured him that they were mine. I was ready for the ax to fall, and I would understand his decision. Dating a young girl with children is a lot to handle. He said something that day that pierced my heart and soul: "Now, I have two girls."

Anthony was like no other boy, man, or person that I had ever met. We began to date, and I believe that I was in love with him at first sight—if not love, certainly a great infatuation. He had brown eyes; he could draw; he was an excellent student; he could roller skate; and he was kind, loving, passionate, affectionate, gentle, thoughtful, caring, and always willing to help others. He was not perfect, but neither was I. He was a blessing to me. In June 1978, I graduated from Hillsborough High School. My parents, family members, and friends were so very proud of my accomplishment. By August 1978, I was starting my freshman year at Bethune Cookman College. On October 25, 1980, I joined my beloved sisterhood, Delta Sigma Theta Sorority, Incorporated, and in April 1984, one of the most important events occurred in my life: I graduated with my nursing degree.

On June 16, 1984, I wed my lover, my best friend, my soulmate, my partner, and my boo. My husband took great care of my heart, our children, and our family. On November 3, 1984, we added another beautiful, healthy baby girl to the family: Antionette Ja-phia Mutcherson, who weighed seven pounds, thirteen ounces. She shared her birthday with her grandmother, Anthony's mom, Mrs. Ollie Mae Mutcherson. In 1985, our marriage was faced with an unthinkable challenge: crack cocaine. The epidemic did not spare us. It was one of the most devastating times in our lives. I was not sure that our marriage would survive the uphill battle. We were challenged daily. We never stopped praying and believing that we would weather the storm. We believed that our love would keep us together forever. I was reminded of the vows we took on June 16, 1984: "I, Cannella Williams, take you, Anthony Ricardo Mutcherson, for my lawful husband, to have and to hold, from this day forward, for better, for worse, for richer, for poorer, in sickness and in health, until death do us part."

On April 26, 1987, we added, yes, another beautiful baby girl to the ever-growing family, Lexie Cannella Mutcherson. Unfortunately, crack cocaine would not go away. It had a grip on my family that was causing us so much distress. My husband's addiction was crippling our family. In 1993, we reluctantly dissolved the marriage. We cried so hard, promising each other that one day we would find our way back together, trying to stop the pain that we were enduring. We never stopped loving one another. We remained good friends.

On April 16, 1995, I remarried an awesome young man, Eric K. Jefferies, and we moved to Tallahassee, Florida. Life can be funny. Both of us are graduates of Bethune Cookman University, now living amongst our archrivals, graduates of FAMU. We have met so many wonderful friends and family members here. Rearing our children in Tallahassee was a blessing for us; we love it here. We also added our beautiful baby girl. My fifth daughter, Malaika Sukari Jefferies, was born August 28, 1996, and finally, my favorite son, Malik Amari Jefferies, was born December 14, 1999. I prayed for him just as my mother prayed for me. My sixth baby. Delayed, but not denied. I'm reminded that in Genesis 1:27, God created man on the sixth day. Thank you, Heavenly Father, for blessing me in the overflow with a loving, Christian, caring, handsome, and hardworking husband; a dedicated family man.

I thank God for the plans that He has for my life. His plans are far greater than I could ever imagine. Life has not always been easy, but God has carried me through each and every challenge. When I was young, uneducated, and impregnated (the title of a poem that my daughter, Antionette, wrote), I could not see beyond my circumstances. I could see God, though. I could see Him show up in my family's grace through His provision and His companionship through the friendships that He blessed me with.

I dedicate this chapter to my loving parents. A special thanks to the two Bettys, and to my Irish twins, Renee and Romekia Brewer.

Young, Uneducated, and Impregnated

Her tears touched her hand that touched her stomach.

Thirteen years of womanhood,

nothing from the norm of her hood,

a baby's dad that was no good.

In fact, he laid her down a year later

to miseducate and impregnate.

Her lesson learned was unlearned.

Again, her tears touched her hand that touched her stomach.

Fourteen years of womanhood,

nothing from the norm of her hood,

a baby's dad that was no good.

In fact, good as gone.

Then, from that day on, she was left to raise and praise two
beautiful children all alone.

Over the years, looked down and persecuted,

with the odds against her, she broke. Even then, she broke free!

Free from the mistakes that took the place of her childhood;

free from the shame that was draped upon her being.

FREE TO BE FREE.

Free to raise my siblings and me.

A woman so strong,

God made stone her backbone.

That sista got it going on!

Her tears touched her hands that

touched her stomach

that have touched my heart.

Thank you, Mom.

I love you.

Antionette 'Toni" Mutcherson

January 10, 2003

Cannella Mutcherson-Jefferies

Chapter 8
God's Pruning

"Pruning removes dead and dying branches and stubs, allowing room for new growth and protecting your property and passerby from damage. It also deters pest and animal infestation and promotes the plant's natural shape and healthy growth."
— *The Grounds Guys*

I thought I was ready, but I guess I wasn't. I made excuses for years as to why I haven't shared these feelings. The main excuse was, "This was way too painful to even deal with if I shared it." Once it was already on paper and I was "freed of it," I felt that was enough. I must mention that this writing journey started in 2012, but it was so painful for me to reabsorb the trauma I experienced (that's what it felt like when I read about it) that sharing my story didn't feel worth it. I remember having so much rage inside of me; I was afraid to read it. Knowing that there are a lot of feelings involved when revisiting my pain, I constantly created a roadblock, using my emotions as an excuse.

I finally got the courage to work on my book in 2014. My new relationship was the inspiration for completion. I finally had someone to support me if I experienced any of these unpleasant emotions while processing, who could also validate me and contradict who I thought I was in my marriage. I had the courage now, and wasn't worried about what my ex thought or if it hurt him one bit, I FINALLY didn't GAF!

...until 2015. We reconciled our friendship, and my "soft little bleeding heart" wouldn't allow me to put all that pain out there when we were speaking and being cordial after five years of silence. Besides, the kids couldn't take another "emotional war," so that was my final excuse for not following through and sharing my experience.

I opened my book, began to read, and got slapped in the face by my past. How could I still be hurting from this? How could I still be THIS angry? More importantly, I began realizing that some of who I was then still resurfaces now, and that was very hard to swallow. I feel trapped, with no way out, and I feel sick. I began asking questions, ruminating, and reflecting on past experiences, and immediately began judging myself. This was going to be hard, and I didn't know where to start or what parts of me to share. I began feeling alone, afraid, and stupid because some parts of this "strong Black woman" who I've aspired to be still had parts of HER inside, and it made me angry. The pain of having to see who I was and still sometimes am prevented me from seeing how far I've come and the lives that I could change by writing.

So, I will begin with the root of it all.

The Root

The roots of me are very deep,

Filled with applications of misinterpretations.

All I FEEL are things that made me weak—

weak in the mind, not on purpose,

but weak because my mom had this way of thinking

she thought was not to hurt, but to protect us.

All the while, inside of me grew many things:

self-judgment, self-hate, but most of all,

low self-esteem.

I had no voice; my opinion was not my own,

and the times when it was, I fell silent, wondering

if it was something anyone even cared to know.

Mom's a Baptist minister, but as a child traumatized.

To her, sheltering us was protecting us every day of our lives.

I couldn't wait to get out

and get on with my life—

get away from church, Jesus, all the nonsense,

which is probably why I prematurely became "wife,"

growing up with something to prove.

I REFUSED TO BE A VICTIM,

not realizing I was already a part of the system.

System of lies and self-judgment; cuz of this, I'd never win.

EVERY FUCKIN' CHOICE I MADE, I had this little voice inside sayin',

THIS IS A SIN!

If I wasn't sinning, I was going to hell.

Pressing pause on dreams, opinions, and ambitions.

For my emotions, no one but me could post bail.

I was scared and afraid, but most of all, confused

I was young, gifted, and Black, for goodness' sake!

But my spirit was bruised.

Fighting with everything in me, I broke away.

Quickly returned home, though, because of what people might say

or think of me:

such a disappointment, not listening to my mom; anything bad was me, I guess.

No matter how much good I did, the bad parts were always being stressed.

I know!

Let me grow up and shine bright like a star.

I got the husband, house, even two kids,

AND that fancy car.

but it still wasn't enough.

I was picture-perfect,

but blemished inside.

But every time I rose up in me,

self-judgment said it was the devil wanting to take me for a ride.

I just wanted to be free,

but what it looked like, I didn't know.

All I knew was I didn't feel whole.

Even with Jesus, husband, business of my own, AND two kids,

I still felt incomplete, despite what I did.

"Wholesome Christian girl" is what I was called,

but was treated the complete opposite.

Adjectives used to describe me would have anyone appalled.

I still get angry at the very thought of it:

fast ass girl who wore tight clothes;

rude, disrespectful, and ignored adults when I was called;

sat in pews with legs wide open to tempt and amuse;

bad influence to other girls, mouthy, and ohhh, yeah—I talked
back, too.

Made to apologize when I didn't even know the cause.

This so-called "village of adults"

were not pointing out mine, but were CREATING FLAWS

about me.

But where was my protector?

My mom?

She was behind the scenes, also trying to survive,

and she trusted other church members with us five.

So I had to grow up,

take care of us, ignore the judgment.

That was one less thing Mom had to do:

fight pointless battles by judgmental Christians

when she had so much other stuff to take care of, too,

like take care of us, because my dad was an addict.

After he got out the military,

he developed a drug habit—

a habit that would cause us to miss out on things,

cause us to go without, and even sometimes homeless.

Growing up seemed like every leftover transgression was mine.

I had to carry it… AND own it.

Find a way to tuck it somewhere deep for it to hide.

And before I knew it… THIS became my life:

carrying everyone's burden,

forsaking myself.

Before I knew it, I was nineteen and taking care of everyone else.

Out of the house, but taking care of family still,

continued forsaking self and giving.

But MY VOID no one cared to fill.

I tried to break free, but this voice in my head

kept repeating over and over,

"Remember what the B.I.B.L.E. says!"

So, again, judgment came to visit me.

Shut down self and all my dreams.

I focused on the me everyone else wanted me to be.

But who is that—or should I say, who *was* it?

I look back now and still get disgusted.

I hate that person, but I love her.

I'm ashamed of her, but glorify her.

All that she was were roots from a damaged tree,

but those experiences, those roots buried so deep,

made me realize that no matter how much I despised

who she was,

still, without her, I couldn't be me.

Who I am now is very important.

I have a story to tell,

for this is a journey I am still on.

All times when I have conquered and failed,

the strength you get from living

and making it through

is an indescribable feeling that nobody understands but GOD
and you.

This journey is intimate, coming from feelings so deep.

Mind silent at times, but through poetry, my heart speaks.

My heart speaks, processes, and oftentimes mends,

but emotional freedom, and closure nonetheless, is what I got in the end.

I'm not sure when the process of reflection began, but all I remember is one day… I woke up.

My subconscious somehow prepared me for what would happen over the next few months. I began contemplating things like my worth, my purpose, my value in life, and what had life given back to me since I had put so much into it. I didn't want to be someone who never reached my full potential because of my circumstances, so I unknowingly began this journey. I say unknowingly because, although I realized my thought process was changing, I didn't realize how quickly my actions would follow. It wasn't easy at first, nor is it still, but along the way I have questioned myself, my sanity, my faith in God, and my purpose in life. Someone once told me, "You have to lose everything in order to gain everything," but of course, **I was different**. My destiny for greatness would not hear of such a thing. I was ignorantly invincible.

I have always worked; I have always been very independent (when it came to business) and goal-driven. I ran a business that allowed me financial freedom at a very young age. You name it, I had it: the house, the husband, and the two children to go with it. I felt like I had done all of the things any responsible person could do to map their way to success, but there was one problem: I had no purpose.

I remember always doing things to make others proud, make others happy, and do what was expected. I made sure I got praised for everything that I did. I liked the feeling of others looking up to me. I felt I already had my place in life (in the eyes of others, that is) because on the inside, I realized I wasn't happy with ME on any level. I thought I could find happiness and fulfillment in work, school, or being a mother. Although I enjoyed those things and was grateful for them, I still didn't feel complete. I tried everything I could to be the best wife any man could ask for, but once again, that was short lived, too. I had only been existing because the purposes I was fulfilling weren't my own. What's ironic is my husband (now ex) and I used to have discussions while lying in bed about where we saw ourselves in our marriage in life one year, three years, and five years from now. We would get excited just off of the discussions we had about our future together. I offered suggestions, he objected to them or modified how I envisioned them, and of course, I went along with his objections and modifications, silently thinking to myself, Why don't you speak up? Why are you letting him change your vision? This would stick with me ... until our next discussion.

Somewhere around 2008, we had *that* discussion again.

My husband asked, "Babe... So, tell me, where do you see us in the next five years?"

I was paralyzed because I didn't expect this question to catch me off guard.

I answered, clearing my throat, "I don't even know if I will be married to you in the next five years."

The look on his face was one of hurt and confusion combined, and he calmly asked, "Why would you say something like that?"

I answered, "Because I don't know who I am or what I want anymore, but I know it's not the same as who you are and what you want."

Of course, the experience of marriage was great, and like any other, it had its ups and downs, from arguments to fighting, not speaking... you know, the typical stuff. There are many things I do not regret, but like the saying goes, "Only if I knew then what I know now would things be so much different." Having the courage to walk away when nothing is perceived as wrong is one of the scariest things imaginable, but something was inside me. Some call it a mid-life crisis, some call it crazy, but whatever it was, it was very profound.

I was grateful for what God had allowed me to accomplish, experience, and learn from, but somewhere in all this gratitude, I still managed to unbury discontentment. I know God doesn't smile on divorce, but I knew no other way out. In my heart, I didn't want to be attached to anything. I contemplated separation or starting my relationship over (with my husband, of course), but I needed a break first to recharge myself, so to speak. I was at a point where everything got on my nerves. The things I had forgiven in the past began to resurface, and I looked at my husband through eyes of resentment instead of love. I remember talking to my mother on many occasions about how I was feeling. She encouraged me to talk to him about it, but every time I tried to bring it up even a little bit, my feelings and thoughts were disregarded. Over time, I adopted the attitude of, "If he does one more thing… I'm leaving." Well, I never got to leave, but after a small pointless disagreement that caused him to come home two weeks early from work (he worked out of town), pack my bags, and put them out because *HE* wasn't going to have a "disrespectful wife," I viewed this as my opportunity.

This small gesture on his part was viewed by me as conditional and controlling, and it demonstrated he had no trust in me. His goal was to control me so that he could remain secure in himself, and I was no longer willing. This act of impulsivity expedited further reflection that would change my life forever.

On April 29, 2009, he wrote a letter to me. This was one of many times I had to process his request to consider the "alternative lifestyle." After reading the email over several times, I found myself telling my husband exactly what he wanted to hear, making sure I always justified it or even validated his feelings along the way, while minimizing mine. Now I ask myself, WHY couldn't I just say what I wanted to say and let him deal with it? Hell! I had to deal with all the things he asked of me and was never validated once! I even ended my email replies to him with "Love, Your Wife (even though you are frustrated with her right now)" because I didn't want to make him mad. I'm disgusted every time I see how weak I was.

We all have desires, fantasies, whatever you want to call them, but the reality of it all is, we don't have to act out everything.

Sadly, my ex-husband's fantasy was exploring his sexual desires with other people, me and other people, "us" and other people, and he tried hard to normalize that for me through constant emails bargaining, convincing, you name it. I wasn't interested in any of it because my only fantasy was pleasing my husband. Now, don't get me wrong, there is nothing wrong with fantasies (if you fantasize and fulfill those fantasies together). Fantasies aren't one sided and should NEVER belittle. I actually think that is the justification for some of the reasons I had a difficult time letting go: I felt like he OWED me something because I felt like he took so much... but did he take it, or did I give it to him?

The Alternative Lifestlye

The alternative lifestyle is what you introduced—

possibly for validation ,a self-esteem boost.

But I thought I was enough; I thought I was your life,

but you still said our relationship needed a little more spice.

The thought of it made my stomach turn,

but soon, I gave in

because the thought of losing you hurt so bad.

I figured, *If you can't beat 'em, join 'em.*

And so... I gave in

to watching you be intimate and passionate with another

woman... Then, you asked if you could watch us with each other.

Ignorance and love convinced me to do it.

ONCE is what you said, one fantasy.

So, I figured I could go through it.

But first, I begged and pleaded,

haunted by second thoughts...

We argued; you ignored me.

After I gave in, we fought.

Then, I became insecure and paranoid in your eyes,

so you decided to fix it

by allowing me to have sex with other guys.

Of course, I was curious

because all I ever had and knew was you…

But you gave me away.

I was scared at first, but then it became easy to do.

Emotionally, you drifted away,

embracing our demise.

An alternative lifestyle is what we had.

This definitely couldn't be wise.

Then, I became lonely

and desired others… not just you.

So, you gave me permission to explore with and without you.

Naive, but curious, I allowed myself to go

off the deep end,

and the love for you I once had… I didn't know.

We both had lost focus.

And then, one day, I would meet

a guy you once gave permission.

With him, I decided to cheat.

I compromised my marriage

and my family, too.

But to think this all started

with one simple request from YOU.

So, you find out... and you make it seem so bad...

The forgiveness I had multiple times for you

for me you never had.

You denounced me as your wife.

Then, to me, all you could say is,

Write a book, bitch, and call it 'Diary of a Cheating Wife.' You disgust me now. Go away."???

Well, that is exactly what I decided to do: write this poem and write this book because it was inspired by you.

Trust and believe, though... one thing you will regret:

throwing me away and talking trash...

This shout-out is the last you'll ever get.

Thank you! Oh, thank you.

Have a nice life,

because I will definitely have one.

I've started over already.

Signed...

Your Cheating Wife

I had no problem being accountable for the role I played in all of this, but it would have meant something at the time for him to acknowledge how he was a major contributor to our failed marriage, or maybe how he failed me as a husband, but I never told him. I'm not sure anymore. I even think to myself sometimes, He never had to tell or show me how to be a good wife, so why did I have to tell him how to be a good husband? The funny thing is, he somehow figured it all out when it was too late. I longed for something that I don't even think he was capable of giving me. My love language was the complete opposite of his, and I often wonder how we stayed together for so long. I just knew I wanted somebody to love me.

I Want Somebody To Love Me

I want somebody to love me who's unconditional and loyal.

I want someone to adore me, hold me, someone willing to spoil.

I want somebody to love me; I'm his only desire.

I want somebody to love me unconditionally, excite me, light my fire.

I want somebody to love me; somebody I can trust.

I want somebody to love me; only for me he will lust.

I want somebody to love me, who can wake up to me every day.

I want the one who loves me to make me his wife someday.

I want somebody to love me; daily, I'm on his mind.

Someone who can't wait to come home to me and spend some quality time.

I want somebody to love me, who also loves my kids.

I want somebody to love them and treat them like they're his.

I want somebody to love back; somebody to come home to.

I want somebody to love me enough to say, "For me, it's only you."

I want somebody to touch me, make me feel alive;

touch every inch of my body, and adore me with his eyes.

I want somebody to hold me when I'm sad or if I cry.

I want somebody to tell me…"I'm glad you're in my life."

I want somebody to love me so strong it makes me weak.

I want somebody to start my sentences before I even begin to speak.

I want somebody to know me and understand my thoughts.

I want somebody who calls me; someone who likes to talk.

Of course, I want experience of love and lots of lust,

but with one person only. I need someone I can trust.

I want somebody to love me, to always keep me safe.

I want somebody who tells me MY heart is his happy place.

I want somebody who loves me for who I am inside.

I want somebody who completes me and needs me in his life.

I want someone to love me and also be my friend.

I want that one who loves me to be there till the end.

Despite how good of a husband he may have *thought* he was, he didn't fit this description by far. THIS was how I wanted to be loved, and it was quite realistic to me. Now that he had released me… I was determined to find it, or let it find me.

The Break-Up

I said I was tired from working all day… spent.

I wanted to take a hot bath and talk to you, and that was it.

We talked on the phone briefly; said you were going to the gym,

but while working out, I got a call from them.

My friends told me, *Get up! Get out!* That's what they said.

Rest later, they told me.

Get out of the bed!

When you called me, I told you I'd be leaving, so text.

Figured you'd want me to get out despite needing rest.

Instead, you got mad, telling me what to do.

All I could do was laugh and say, *I don't take orders from you.*

You said, *Go… You'll be sorry. This is something you'll definitely regret.*

But away I went anyway… Your threat I'd quickly forget.

At the party, you harassed me, making me feel bad;

guilt-tripping me, playing mind games, making me feel sad.

So, I got my stuff, went home,

decided to give in

to honor my husband's request

and not hang out with my friends,

thinking changing my mind

would work out for the best,

not realizing the next day

what would happen next.

I went to the store.

At home, I left your kids.

Then, our daughter texted me, saying,

Mom, guess what Dad did…

He came home early from work,

packed all of your stuff,

said you were bad, and had to leave us.

I was instantly mad, holding back tears with all of my might.

Seeing my stuff in trash bags outside

made me want to fight,

BUT

I kept my composure and spoke to my kids.

Told them it wasn't their fault—

it was something I did.

Now, I had time to think.

What was I going to do?

One thing I knew right away was…

I'm not coming back to you.

How dare you throw out my things

like I was some trash?

No benefit of the doubt;

no questions you'd ask.

You just acted impulsively—

packed my things and put them out,

forgetting the unconditional love I showed to you

year in and year out.

No, I was not perfect, but you were not, either.

But this statement you just made

made our relationship even weaker.

Now, I was ready to leave you,

not to look back.

Living life not married to you?

Many times, I'd contemplated just that.

You made it so easy when you put me out.

Thought you were sending a message,

but now, you had doubts

that I would come back cuz of the stunt that you did.

So, you figured you'd get me to come using our kids.

At first, it worked.

Then, I would discover

we'd have to divorce,

then co-parent with each other.

Difficult at first; our kids had to adjust,

but leaving you had to happen... definitely a must.

The message you sent on that Super Bowl Sunday

was unconditional love... had long gone away.

Now, though this trial was definitely bad,

I can only reflect... on WHAT WE HAD...

GETTING OUR LIFE BACK

Your proposal to me

was to get our life back.

You began by admitting that you acted unfair

for putting my things out

and acting like you didn't care.

You tried to convince me by admitting your wrongs.

When I asked why you wanted me back,

your reply was, *That's where you belong*—

Not, *Because I love you; because you are my wife,*

not, *Because I can't imagine you out of my life.*

All your reasons were selfish,

did not include me,

and all I could think was

I wanted to be free—

free of you and the obligation of being your wife,

because when you threw me away,

I reflected on life:

the life I had given you

while compromising mine,

knowing I had to leave you

would be hard at first, but I would be fine.

I let you talk and express what you had to say,

but I still had to tell you I wasn't coming home with you today.

I could feel the pain in your heart,

see the hurt in your eyes.

You'd be lost without me

being a part of your life.

I had to be strong

and admit we had grown apart.

We were different people now.

We needed a new start.

I know hearing that broke you; I could see all your hurt.

But I proposed we'd start over—

dating each other—

see if that worked.

You denied my request,

said we needed no time alone.

Any problems we had

we would fix with me home.

That's not what I wanted.

That wasn't my plan.

I decided not to return,

not to have you as my man.

We talked friendly often.

I thought we would be friends.

What reality would now show me—

here's where hostility begins.

First, you started insulting me through text.

Then came emails and phone calls.

Phone stalking would be next.

You tried to get my attention the best way you could,

thinking intimidation might work,

and initially… it would.

I grasped my anxiety,

reclaimed my emotional health,

screaming inside all the while,

YOU ARE STRONG!!!

Get a hold of yourself.

You hurt me at first; your words made me cry

because you knew me so well.

Now, about me, you would lie.

To our friends and our family, my name you would slander,

thinking you'd hurt me by destroying my character.

But don't worry, baby… I will be back on top.

Success, using God-given talents,

something you're not ordained to stop.

You've put up your obstacles... roadblocks.

You think you are clever,

but God-given talents

you can't take away—EVER.

Now, wishing, praying daily your misery would end.

It's self-inflicted, sorry…

On your knees now, you're repenting again and again

for God to have mercy on your soul and your life

for treating me so bad… your used-to-be wife.

Ahead of you a long road,

many things you'll discover.

One thing you should do, though:

Please take along your mother,

so she, too, can realize the influence

she had on your life—

helping you lose your entire family,

your kids, your best friend, your wife.

The Rage

Once the anger set in, I began to vent. I vented things I never thought my heart would allow my mind to think or my mouth to say. Of course, after hurt and pain, everyone has thoughts that are filled with anger. It was almost like a grieving process, only I wasn't grieving the end of my marriage—I was grieving the life I never felt I had. At this point, I was mad, hurt, and trying to find the reason for my long-term stupidity. Reading the past emails between us only confirmed how selfish and self-centered the person I had sacrificed so much for was. I never said I was perfect, but I damn sure was close! Well, there is no explanation necessary for what you are about to read because it comes straight from the heart, to the mind to be expressed with words. In his eyes, I had already been replaced. A memory forgotten; an experience erased. How could this be? Maybe this is how he heals: Reject me, disrespect me, then substitute me with someone else. I can only feel sorry for the woman who has to fill my shoes. I will always pray for him trying to find someone qualified enough to fill them. She will definitely be an unsuspecting victim of HIS circumstance because I am definitely healing.

I had lost my innocence to my husband at the age of fifteen years old. He was eighteen years old. I was not necessarily in a rush, nor did I have a desire to lose it the day that I did, but I had figured, *Well, I like him, so I guess.* This thought process was not a healthy one, and the only other experiences I had with other men were the ones we engaged in during the time of our open marriage, and that was four. BUT the unfortunate thing is, I never learned how to interact with a man, and I only knew what I had been engaging in was not love. There was no passion involved, just the experience of being with someone who needed to "get off," so to speak. These relationships (or encounters) piqued my interest in many ways because I was inexperienced. I was very curious about many things and naive about much more. This mixture led me on a path of destruction. Maybe my ex feels I cheated because in the midst of our open relationship, I began having sexual relations with someone HE introduced me to, but this time, I did it without his permission. I just had gotten to a point where I just didn't care. So, YES... I was unfaithful, BUT I had only been unfaithful to my husband the last six months of our seventeen-year relationship. No, this doesn't excuse my adulterous behavior, but it just provides confirmation for me that I am capable of sustaining a relationship and being faithful. I say all that to say once I had no marital obligation, I did not know how to act with men. I didn't know when to give my heart to someone, nor could I recognize when I was being used, taken for granted, or just plain stupid. I was single and looking for someone to see me for the WOMAN I had become and was becoming. I had no idea that there were men out there who had been in the game for so long that having ill intentions was the norm, and I was not smart enough to recognize it. So, I did what I knew to do to get a hold of myself and stop the foolishness because THIS was not who I was. So, again, I went to God, spoke from my heart, and asked for what I really wanted.

My Man

My man is loving, kind, and true.
Exclusively in love, I'm his only desire.
The love he has for me continuously lights my fire.

My man is unconditional; he loves me for better or worse.
Nothing I ever say or do will deter him... and he makes me
second in his life... only because he makes God first.
My man prays with me, encourages me, and speaks life to all
that I do, because all my talents are God-given and he knows
they will benefit him, too.
My man anticipates my needs, even before I know what they
are, because he talks daily to God, who shows him my heart.
My man adores me. I am the apple of his eye. We are made for
each other... God's gift.. an unbreakable bond... he and I.
My man loves me like God instructs a man to do: Love her like
Christ loves the church, loving me freely. God's way doesn't

182

take very much work.
My man comforts me when I'm stressed and whispers in my ear when I'm discouraged, reminding me I am blessed and he is here.
My man is monogamous; he only has eyes for me. When I look back into his eyes, it's GOD's reflection I see.
My man thinks of me days, sometimes nights, for no specific reason. He buys cards, flowers, and gifts, no matter the holiday or season.
My man is gentle, affectionate, and selfless when making love. My man is very prideful, but also humble, recognizing his strength comes from God above.
My man is hard-working, a provider, and very wise.
My man puts God first in all that he does, and then he loves his wife.
My man is my desire, my man is God's will... My man, next to God, has some big shoes to fill.

Trust God

Telling GOD the desires of my heart is where I began this journey of mine. I have experienced marriage, heartbreak, and heartache. I realize that the one commonality in all my experiences is my need for substance, BUT I was chasing emptiness. In order to achieve complete happiness, I needed to prepare myself mentally, emotionally, and spiritually for what GOD had in store for me. CHANGE IS GOOD! At this very moment, I am single, and still waiting on God to build my husband so he can find me. Along the way, I have strayed in impatience out of loneliness and even desperation at times. Sometimes, I even got angry, wondering why God was taking so long to come for me, especially when it seemed like He was so readily blessing everyone else. But I had to get out of my head. God sees all of me, all of my needs, and He already knows how impatient I am and will be. All the while, He is still preparing me for the man He has for me and only me. I've rushed Him in the past, and the consequences of me taking over were heartache and heartbreak because the men I've met have never seen me through the lens that God wants me to be seen through. I think my fear of growing old alone has caused me to get in my own way sometimes. This journey has required me to reflect more and hold myself accountable in areas I thought I already had. I believe my husband will find me through my elevation, which means I still have fears to conquer and things to learn so that I will wind up in that place of excellence God is preparing me for. And when I get to that place, my husband will be there waiting, seeing me through the eyes of God.

As I continue to grow and come to resolve with my past experiences, finding closure also means accepting what has happened, being accountable for the role I played regardless of how I was influenced, forgiving myself, and moving forward. Being set free, to me, means no longer being bound, knowing in my heart I am forgiven and because of God's grace and mercy. I have overcome, and because of all I have been through, I now know I am here because I am healed!

Sha'rron Cross

Chapter 9
Scar Tissue

Scar Tissue. (*skar-TIH-shoo*)

Noun. *Dysfunctional connective tissue that forms in the human body when normal tissue is destroyed by disease, injury, or surgery.*

I was ten or eleven years old the first time I began writing, "I hate you. You're ugly. You're fat. Die." The "You" was me; I was talking to myself. Now, I would guess that if you are reading this, your first thought is, "Why?" There was no significant event; there was no abuse, I was not raised in poverty, and I was not raised in a family with sadistic ideologies or traditions. In fact, my childhood was quite the opposite. But there was a point when I became melancholy.

The German philosopher Friedrich Nietzsche characterized the spirit of melancholy as a demon. It reaches so deeply into the roots of human existence there is an implication that the state of being melancholy exceeds what we can learn through the studies of psychology and psychiatry. Melancholy conveys the idea of heaviness of spirit. It rests like a weight pressing down, blinding all sense of clarity, binding everything that otherwise acts freely, that otherwise moves and produces results, thus weakening the mastery of one's own life.

As early as I can remember, I was a happy, friendly, inquisitive, creative, and, quite honestly, *very* intelligent child. I should have been all of these things, considering that my parents had been married for seven years before they had me, and only me. An aunt of mine jokes that she worried I may have *never* made it on the scene, considering the amount of pets my parents had prior to my birth. Maybe they weren't sold on the idea of having a child, who knows.

But I do know that they were led by Christian morals, financially stable, and equipped to be parents. In return, this provided me with access to culture, extracurricular activities, a firm foundation in faith, safety, and a stable life.

Only children get a bad rap. Obviously, I cannot relate to the woes or benefits of siblings, but I will say that if the assumption is that being an only child indicates being spoiled, I would argue that it can also be a tremendous burden to bear. Hear me out. Siblings have the opportunity to play multiple roles during their lives, which, from my perspective, balances the amount of attention received for any good or bad thing. I, on the other hand, am all the things to my parents: the smart child, the creative child, the super hard-headed child, the black sheep child, the funny child, the pretty child. I could go on, but you get the point. And yes, the last description was necessary to mention.

As my parents get older and approach fifty years of marriage, I find that my thoughts often examine the extraordinary idea that our parents are hand-picked, no matter what. Perhaps it is because I am a single parent now, and some things will never resonate until you experience them for yourself. What I know for sure is that children are born *through* us, not to us. Who they become will always belong to God. I have also learned to consider that our parents held identities before we were born. I'd like to think that who they were prior to our existence was an intricate detail in a master plan to create the perfect genealogical ancestry and genetic inheritance, which is necessary for us to complete our unique and specific purpose on earth.

One could say that I am a Daddy's girl. When you couple that with being an only child, it is safe to say that my dad worked overtime. Both of my parents worked hard, but he, in particular, labored with long and rotating shifts that wore his physical body down. He never let the weight of his work duties and anything else I wasn't privy to as a child stop him from being a very present and providing father—a father who didn't have a father. A phenomenal faith-filled father.

I remember certain details of my kindergarten graduation like yesterday—mainly that I was supposed to practice singing certain lines to a song so that when it was my turn to go to the microphone, I'd be prepared to perform.

I can see the cobblestone fireplace of my parents' den and the light tan pillow my Daddy used to sit on. I'd burst past him, bouncing around in all my four-year-old energy, saying, "Daddy, will you sing my part again?" He'd belt out the lyrics that I had been assigned in a fantastic tenor bravado, and I'd joined in, singing my heart out. Moments like that always stay with me.

Around the third grade, I was *dedicated* to rise into softball stardom. I'd see the other girls change out of their school clothes and into their uniforms for ball games after school, and *sincerely resented* my inexperience playing a sport that, by all accounts, was a rite of passage in the south.

Looking back, I'm compelled to believe that my mom influenced this opportunity, but at the time, all I saw was my daddy entertaining the idea of me actually hitting the ball by throwing some pitches in the front yard. I put on all my gear, and with shorts rolled up, I mustered my toughest look and put batting gloves on each hand with the *utmost* theatrics. I swiveled my bat around like I'd seen in every cartoon, and in my mind, it was going *down*. I stood under my parents' pear blossom tree, and he pitched the ball, soft and sweet. I swung with the might of Hercules—and I probably shut my eyes, knowing me—but I hit nothing but air. He threw it again, but I missed it. After about ten pitches of placating my dreams, and him looking at me trying with all my might, he softened the pitch even more. Every time the wind from my swing set me back, his response was, "Mmm." Now, see, that was petty, because Black folks' vernacular consists of the same word that can mean many things. Back then, it was definitely, "MMM!" ...As in, "She ain't got it, not with this bat and ball!"

In a very well-played parental move, my dad took a big stretch, followed by, "Whew! I'm tired. Let's go inside and get out this heat." I am certain that he was being respectful of my feelings, but he also decided not to waste our time. From age eight forward, *anytime* I mentioned sports, he'd say, "Oh, no! You don't want to hurt your hands. Protect them." On one hand, he was referring to my budding talent as a musician, but it was also reverse psychology at its finest. I didn't even realize how well he played me until I was deep into adulthood.

Like any good parent, my daddy guided and affirmed me in the areas I excelled. He always showed up to support me—when I didn't expect it, when I needed him the most, and when I knew I needed him, but didn't want him to.

And by His grace, it is possible to believe that God is perfect in all of His ways. It is possible for us, even in our unwanted circumstance, to not want; because we have all that we need in our good, good Father.

"The Lord is my shepherd; I shall not want.[2] He makes me to lie down in green pastures; He leads me beside the still waters.[3] He restores my soul; He leads me in the paths of righteousness For His name's sake.[4] Yea, though I walk through the valley of the shadow of death, I will fear no evil; For You are with me; Your rod and Your staff, they comfort me.[5] You prepare a table before me in the presence of my enemies; You anoint my head with oil; My cup runs over.[6] Surely goodness and mercy shall follow me All the days of my life; And I will dwell in the house of the Lord Forever." — Psalm 23:1–6 (NKJV)

Beyond our upbringing and background, or who may or may not have raised us, we all have experiences that define who we are. This certainly rings true of my experience as a musician and the artistic work of performance so core to my identity. I began taking piano lessons at four years old. As my gift developed, I transformed into a competitive classically trained pianist. However, music, in its most simplistic and vulnerable form, helped shape my personality during my formative years.

My daddy was always singing, and my ear-gates were fortified with great music from artists like Andraé Crouch, The Winans, and Commissioned. I never knew anything different, or that it was, to some, different. So, naturally, I began to do the same, completely unaware that I was practicing the ability to express emotions through art. I don't think I have one memory that is not enveloped with a certain sound indicative of the moment and the feelings it rendered. Music was my first vehicle of expression.

And I would use it to share my identity, connect my stories with others, and convey my injuries.

When you injure yourself, scar tissue develops as part of the normal healing process. Scars look and act differently than the healthy skin that surrounds them. Usually, they are just plain ugly.

It is ironic to think that scars, the evidence of healing, can also cause pain. Unlike healthy tissue, scar tissue forms in random, criss-crossing patterns. It is not as flexible or as functional as the tissue that it is replacing. It has poor circulation, which limits the supply of fresh oxygen and nutrients. Not only is scar tissue weak, it can impede movement and overall performance, making it prone to reinjury.

I attended a private Christian school with an extensive academic curriculum for the majority of my life. Most of my activities outside of the classroom also required a high standard of discipline to excel. Some may have categorized me as being gifted back then, but my ability to focus and remain disciplined was, in part, the result of being completely naïve to the world around me and practicing to perform under pressure. This conditioning developed a muscle that purposed me to maintain a level of excellence so that when the light shone on me, I, too, was prepared to shine.

Like most church kids, I grew up sheltered. I was raised in southern Alabama and spent a lot of time in predominantly white spaces where feelings of isolation and exclusion were all too familiar. I realize that Black students can sometimes thrive in these spaces, but there *are* social ramifications that can have adverse effects. As I experienced.

I was usually the only Black person in my entire grade up until the eighth grade. As other kids focused on their get-togethers and vacation trips, tattling on about who liked who, I found that my presence was less than tolerated. Unaccompanied in my attempts to balance the different thoughts in my head about what others thought about me and how I could carry myself in a way that was pleasing, I began to focus on the pounds of weight that I was gaining and how terrible and disgusting my weight gain made me feel inside and out. While my size had everything to do with the quantity of what I ate and how little I exercised, it was also the external manifestation of extreme stress while attempting to be perfect in the face of microaggressions.

Oftentimes, my peers came to school repeating the hateful and intolerant remarks they had heard from their parents, spewing their vitriol onto me and without consequence. One girl went so far as to repeatedly call me a nigger in a full-on berate during recess. What I remember the most were the stares. Some of the kids snickered in laughter, covering their mouths as they said who-knows-what to one another. Others just looked on. Maybe they were waiting for a reaction from me. I'll never know.

I remember running up the hill in a frenzy to find my teacher to tell her what happened. She listened, and as my eyes gazed into hers, full of emotion, her disposition slipped into a blank stare. She casually turned her head to the side as if I had said nothing at all. I repeated myself, assuming that she must not have heard me. This time, she didn't acknowledge my presence or my voice, and simply looked away. I stood there for a while, confused by it all. My head and shoulders shrunk down. In a rather caustic manner, it was unequivocally unforgettable moments like these that created an unexpected layer of resiliency within me. I have never forgotten these moments. And I never expected that I would possess such strength.

Did you know that some scar tissue will never go away? Long after the short-term effects of injury, scars may gradually become smoother and softer, even fading for a period of two years. It is unlikely that scars will fade after this time. This does not mean that you have to live with damaged tissue the rest of your life. If treated properly, the injured tissue can be remodeled to resemble normal, healthy tissue. This will reduce pain and restore normal behavior in any area of the body.

I begged a thousand times over to leave that school. While I gained a scholastic foundation, excelling in fine arts and oratory competitions, I lost any real sense of identity, love, and appreciation for simply being me. By seventh and eighth grade, most of the girls I went to school with became intensely focused on being thin. I distinctly remember a chapel meeting with all the female students in what must have been the fifth through the twelfth grade. I was completely lost as to why we were all sitting in a special session with teachers and administrators—and, furthermore, why they were making a pointed effort to advise us to eat. I asked an after-school teacher what it all meant, but she laughed and said it was nothing I had to worry about. She was right—not eating had never been my problem.

As my eighth grade year came to a close, I was finally free to attend public high school. I knew I didn't fit in at my private school, but boy, was I in for a surprise if I thought that high school would be an easy adjustment.

I remember my first marching band practice. It was held on a summer evening, and this experience introduced me to my freshman year. In the south, when day folds into night, there is a sound. The crickets get loud. The see-saw of their wings rubbing together becomes a united string section. The bellows of frogs take over the bass line, and staccato-like inflections from one creature or another take part in leading the low-humming orchestra.

As the sun set into the skyline across the track of my high school campus, this sound reverberated across the landscape. Outdoor lights began to glimmer, lighting up the pathway to the band room. My wardrobe consisted of knee-length shorts in accordance with my previous school's dress code. Nervously, I hopped out of my parents' car that night wearing just that, with tube socks stretched upward toward my knees, shirt tucked in, and a mouth full of braces accenting my smile.

I attended a 6A high school, and the band was huge. Chairs upon chairs wrapped around a single pedestal where I knew my instructor would stand. While other students laughed and greeted each other, I walked around, silently searching for my last name on a seat in the trumpet section. I was at least fifteen minutes early to this first practice, but after finding my seat and knowing no one to talk to, I pulled out my instrument and began shining it to at least appear unafraid.

A shift occurred, and the buzz of students talking lulled into a hush. When I looked up, everyone had found their place, and we all sat there in silence for a solid ten minutes until the instructor left his office. A gray-haired man walked to the podium. Stale in face, he gazed at the room. With baton in hand, he ushered us, in a semicircular movement, to lift our instruments.

"C," he said.

In his next baton movement, as all musicians understand, we bellowed into our instruments, sustaining it until the instructor, with the same semicircular movement of the baton, advised us to stop. It was one of the most exhilarating musical moments I had ever experienced. I was well accustomed to performing piano solos, but this sound was huge! This sound was incredible, and the breadth of it all moved me to acknowledge that a refinement in my existence had occurred. I had become a part of something, and my sound mattered.

When school started, I was excited to join a student body that represented every race, nationality, and creed. I quickly ran for student government president of our freshman class and won. This was a temporary moment where it seemed I had reached new heights and acceptance, but, like most things, it was short-lived.

There was so much that I had never been exposed to beyond the confines of my parents' home, school, scheduled activities, church, and immediate family. As impossible or irrational as it may seem, I never heard cursing before high school. I knew what curse words *were*, but with little exposure to secular music, movies, or television shows where this was the norm, it was beyond me.

I will never forget the language, disrespect for authority, and aptitude for physical violence I witnessed from some of the students the first week of high school. As someone who was taught in my previous academic environment that saying, "Oh, my gosh," was blasphemy, I can honestly say that I was in a state of horror and culture shock. While I was bright academically, with none of my classes posing a challenge, I was also socially awkward and a "mark," once again, for being different from my peers.

I wasn't socialized to the normalcies of the time, nor was I aware that how I spoke, dressed, or styled my hair was outside the norm. The high school experience that started off promising became a mirror of voices reaffirming the idea that my differences and unique identity were not okay.

My sophomore year, I adjusted from my little girl appearance with bows in her hair to my best attempt at appearing to fit in. There were a handful of people that I held commonalities with who I was able to build a degree of friendship with, but I was never the person who belonged to any particular group. I managed to navigate the social circles of the people in my classes and extracurricular activities, but more often than not, I remained an easy subject for comedic relief, and at my expense. I never complained, as it seemed a social strike worth bearing as long as I didn't have to exist in the same isolation that I'd experienced at my other school. At that time, I valued the social interaction more than I was equipped to recognize the cumulative effect that these hurtful and disrespectful relationships would have on me, magnifying my already-distorted body image and the continual tearing down of my self-esteem.

By the end of my sophomore year, my social survival began to cost too much. I had peers that called me "friend," but those relationships were contingent upon me accepting my position as the target of their jeers, not voicing my thoughts or opinion, and, on some occasions, keeping secrets that I knew were wrong. So, I stopped talking—literally. I stopped interacting and started wandering the halls before school, during lunch, and any other time I could have spent socializing. During class, I became engrossed in what was actually being taught, while some of my peers mumbled amongst themselves at the change in my behavior. When that school year ended, with my regular straight-A report card, I had enough. My internal being had suffered from muting who I was as a person and muting my voice. In the solitary confinement of my mind, there was no ease of understanding the thoughts in my head, nor the distress from my experiences. I was disillusioned toward creating a new version of myself that was pleasing. Operating without the accompaniment of wisdom and deceived down a path of self-reliance, I failed to consider God.

"Oh, yes, you shaped me first inside, then out; you formed me in my mother's womb. I thank You, High God—You're breathtaking! Body and soul, I am marvelously made! I worship in adoration—what a creation! You know me inside and out, You know every bone in my body; You know exactly how I was made, bit by bit, how I was sculpted from nothing into something. Like an open book, You watched me grow from conception to birth; all the stages of my life were spread out before You, The days of my life all prepared before I'd even lived one day." — Psalms 139:13 (MSG)

"The human body is not just a human body. It is an extraordinary work of art by the God of all creation. Each one of us is individually handcrafted, and there is something fearful about how we have been made. This does not change when we grow up. It is a unique work of art. No matter how we might be tempted to see ourselves, God actually sees us in a very different kind of way." — Sam Allberry

The summer of my sophomore year, I decided to take control. While I managed to slim down some throughout my transition from private school to high school, I was still overweight. I found a solution for my self-hate and what I thought I *could* control about what others thought about me—my weight. I had no understanding of nutrition or working out at that time, but I knew that the girls at my previous school changed their appearance quickly and were adored for their quick "glow-ups," even though they were achieved by not eating or by vomiting whatever food they did eat.

I loved food, so by all accounts, not eating was not an option. I decided to try the alternative.

In my home life, whatever my mother prepared, I ate. The

first day I chose to vomit my meal to lose weight, I snuck into my parents' master bathroom and let it go. It was terrible. Every voice in my head said to stop, but I was so sickened and consumed by it all that it felt like forcefully purging my feelings and my food couldn't hurt any worse. In my mind, if I had to go to such lengths, I was creating a worthwhile outcome—and it would be one that would make my appearance better and my life easier. I thought that this would change others' behavior toward me, and to a degree, it did. But not without consequence. The more you try to control something, the more it controls you.

I knew that my pattern of going to the bathroom after meals would not continue to go unnoticed, so I came up with another plan. Since riding my bike around the neighborhood was not out of the norm to my parents, I folded paper towels, stuffed them in my shirt, and began taking rides to exercise after my meals. As my weight began to quickly and noticeably drop, I began making intentional remarks, stating, "I'm about to work this meal off and exercise." *Yeah, right.*

This excuse generally got me out of the house without question, but that wasn't exactly what I was up to. I grew up riding the hills and trails throughout my suburban neighborhood since I was old enough to ride, and I used that knowledge to navigate my quest. I exercised, all right—by ripping around the corner from my parents' home straight to a cul-de-sac where I hopped the curb and followed through to the woods. The tires of my bike tore through the terrain, eventually creating a trail of my own that led to a group of trees. I found a flat spot that seemed safe and did my business. No one but the crickets and the trees could hear me gagging, no one could easily walk up without me hearing, and if anyone found the evidence, they wouldn't associate it with me. I did that every day as I found it necessary. By the time school rolled around again, I began my junior year at five feet, four inches tall and 106 pounds. I know because I weighed myself every day.

Scar tissue is not made from the same great material you were born with, and the pain may vary from individual to individual. While it may be more apparent in some immediately after the formation of the scar, others may start experiencing it much later in life. Some individuals may even start experiencing pain after the complete healing of the scars due to later involvement of nerves. Another major cause of scar tissue pain is the damage caused by deep wounds and burns to the bones and joints underneath. This may present as a "deeply" felt pain at the scarring sites.

In the cases of internal injuries and trauma, scar tissue may replace the healthy tissues inside. As the scarring worsens and time goes on, the pain and discomfort felt by the individual may also worsen.

No one really said anything about my weight loss at school. Instead, I began receiving backhanded compliments like, "You look so much better now," or, "Wow, I didn't know you were so pretty." At least part of my plan had worked. At school, my outer appearance was not a source of pain, but inwardly, I had reached new heights of extreme anxiety and depression. Where I had cast myself into isolation in an effort to avoid my peers before, it had now become a requirement to function.

Eating disorders rarely develop as a result of the weight. While those who suffer are consumed with the imperfections of their outer appearance, their motivation can be in part to physically stem or even reverse their development into adulthood. Many professionals would argue that at the root, eating disorders are the physical manifestation of anxiety and control disorders that perfectionists are typically prone to. The preoccupation has less to do with being thin, but having enough discipline to control your own body, counterbalancing trauma.

The landscape of my high school was an outdoor campus. During breaks and lunch periods, students gathered in groups on the sidewalks and walls of the building to gossip and talk about whatever was relevant to the teenage mind at that time. Because of this setup, for others to pass by, it was a bit of a runway. In my case, navigating through this sea of people brought about unsolicited attention and fear. I couldn't do it. I wouldn't. My legs would shake, my hands would tremble, and I was terrified that if I did make it past the different cliques of high school hierarchy, I would either pass out, or trip and fall on my face. I should point out that I am indeed a klutz, so this was a real-life possibility. I didn't know that what I was experiencing—feeling time convert into slow motion, noticing my breath getting short, and hearing the cadence of my heart rate increase—was extreme anxiety, nor did I know that I would still be wrestling with it to this day. If this type of fear and negative thinking pattern is not confronted and challenged, anxiety will emerge into an all-consuming handicap that disrupts your daily life.

I continued to walk the halls during designated breaks day after day until I found that the auditorium was not locked. There, I could absorb myself in playing a grand piano that sat offstage. By this time, I was really advanced in my performance skills and would utilize the echo and vibrato of the room to wear out whatever sonata or classical movement my piano instructor had assigned. I also began to develop my capacity to play by ear and enjoyed singing and playing ballads from the latest R&B charts. Every now and again, a person here or there would hear me in the auditorium and befriend me at least for the moments that I was playing. Music can do that—it will bring the oddest of people together. It can create or change the tone of emotions, establishing an understanding and appreciation that goes beyond words.

While I continued to suffer inwardly, struggling to master my weight, I became widely known at school as the girl who played the piano—a social identity that I was proud of. With the continuum of my deceitful behavior, compounded by my alarming and irresponsible weight loss, life at home was a different story. My parents had become hip to my tricks that insisted upon trips to the bathroom after meals, and they did their best to block my every move. You may be wondering why the purging behavior continued if I lost the weight that I was so consumed with. While starvation breeds quick results, it does not provide long-term weight loss. Once you start eating again, the weight returns, and so does the never-ending cycle on the body and the mind. We are not always equipped to see the cost of our decisions on the front end. In fact, you may only see the positive, as I did. That is deception.

"Stop deceiving yourselves. If you think you are wise by this world's standards, you need to become a fool to be truly wise." — 1 Corinthians 3:18 (NLT)

My junior year, I won my first pageant. Not everyone was happy. After begging my parents to allow me to participate, I made every effort to handle most things on my own because I knew I could win. I borrowed an evening gown from a classmate who was well-known for winning pageant titles across the state. This wasn't a bad move. The fact that I borrowed an evening gown from someone who barely weighed 100 pounds made it a bad move. In spite of my best efforts to fit into that dress, the gig was up at home, and there was nothing I could do to decrease my 115-pound frame before the big day. The gown fit, but it was still snug around my rib cage. Somehow, I came up with the bright idea to wrap packing tape tightly around my waist to solve the problem. Now, technically, this could have and would have worked, but I made the mistake of using double-sided tape. Whatever you are thinking while reading this, the answer is yes. I made it through the beginning of the evening gown competition gracefully, but with slow and eventual gusto, the dress began to stick to the tape from the inside, making a very large crease that I could not smooth. As a result, I stood on stage and buckled between grasping at my waist to cover the imperfection and holding my posture straight.

Neither the audience nor the judges could deny that I was well-spoken after I proved my intelligence in the interview portion and tore the house down with my piano performance. Since the talent and speech components of the pageant weighed the most in scoring, *easily*, I won. Of course, when the judges announced my name as the victor taking the crown, in the *one moment* I should have used one hand to balance my crown and the other to hold my scepter, I nervously and self-consciously jerked my arms back and forth from my waist back up to my crown in what surely looked like a poor attempt at doing "the robot." This added to some of the audience's disapproval that I had won. I was the most underestimated and least confident participant in that pageant. But what I held *on the inside*, regardless of my physical appearance, took the crown and won.

The next week at school, some bright star thought it necessary to announce my new pageant title during student announcements. This resulted in a low mumble that could be heard across hallways. I remember shrinking down in my desk, my face immediately getting hot, and refusing to make eye contact with anyone as my peers whispered all around me. I continued to walk the halls and hide in the auditorium during breaks and lunch that day.

When my senior year arrived, I had a 4.125 GPA. I applied to every college I could think of and was accepted to all. My weight loss tapered off, but not because I had improved my self-esteem or my relationship with food. I discovered diet pills. As it remains true today, many diet supplements are not approved by the Federal Drug Administration. Back then, these items relied heavily on the now-banned herb, ephedra, to suppress the appetite and increase metabolism to burn fat. Ephedra also posed serious safety risks, including injury, illness, and death. Since it was impossible for me to get away with purging anymore, having used every scheme in the book for the previous two years, I began taking the over-the-counter diet pills. This allowed me to float under my parents' radar, deflecting from my previous behavior. I was now positioned to eat very little while not experiencing hunger pains, allowing me to maintain my ideal weight.

The opposite of scar tissue or physical deformity that spoils the completeness of something is wholeness. Nobody wants to be flawed. Nobody says that, "When I grow up, I want to live in a state of constant melancholic depression." Nobody wants to fail and grow up feeling defeated. We were never meant to drown in self-doubt. Wilt thou be made whole?

"Now, a certain man was there who had an infirmity thirty-eight years. [6] When Jesus saw him lying there, and knew that he already had been in that condition a long time, He said to him, 'Do you want to be made well?' [7] The sick man answered Him, 'Sir, I have no man to put me into the pool when the water is stirred up; but while I am coming, another steps down before me.' [8] Jesus said to him, 'Rise, take up your bed, and walk.' [9] And immediately the man was made well, took up his bed, and walked." — John 5:1–2 (NKJV)

Throughout my junior and senior years, I began spending more and more time with an aunt and a cousin who was close to my age. Even though I didn't spend a lot of time with my aunt when I was younger, there are unforgettable moments etched in my memory. In my hometown, the high schools held a prom procession ceremony at our local civic center that allowed family and friends to view the attendees being escorted by their dates, presenting each student to society one by one. Yes, I, too, realize how deeply rooted I was in southern tradition after writing that.

At about nine years old, I joined my family in the stands to watch one of my eldest cousins escort his date. Now, I am compelled to say that "Save the Best for Last" by Vanessa Williams was humming softly in the background, because what else could have been playing that was so sentimental it moved me to tears? I shake my head and laugh at my own self when I think about it. I can't fully explain what I was feeling, but as the tears burned down my cheeks watching it all, I must have sniffled audibly because my aunt looked down and wrapped her arm around my shoulder, pulling me close. She looked at me, her own eyes welling up with tears, and said, "I know, baby. It makes me want to cry, too." It was like we were in a bubble of empathy all on our own.

She was always kind, and in the time I spent with her, she went out of her way to offer me the best treats, chocolates, and candies any kid could ask for. I always declined. Looking back, I recognize that in her own subtle way, she was trying to get me to eat.

That spring, as the end of my senior year drifted atop of the horizon, I experienced a rare glimpse at the sacred gift and brevity of life. Death brings an understanding into perspective that life is special. My aunt was loving and attentive; subtle, yet purposeful; and, in all her ways, she encouraged me to heal. As quickly as I had been given the time to grow closer to her, she was gone.

Charles Spurgeon, known as the "Prince of Preachers," said, "Jesus wept, but he never complained." While all things are not in our control, and we do not have the power to change the past, go back in time, and change the things that happened to us or the things that people did to us, what we have been gifted with is freedom in forgiveness.

Survival is one thing, and certainly, it is a testament to our strength, but it is a foolish idea to think that staying in any one state without continued growth is the full will of God for our lives. Individuals who suffer a physical injury can heal with medical care, but scarring of the wound is part of the healing process. If you suffer a burn, in the most severe of cases, skin grafts may be taken from other areas of the body, ointments applied, and a scheduled changing of bandages put into regimen to ensure that the wounds heal without infection. However, the more severe the burn, the more noticeable the scar. All scars after an injury cannot physically be seen. How you are injured can play a role.

As I got older, my history with food, fluctuating weight, and poor self-image led me to a healthier approach and an intense focus on fitness and nutrition. Initially, I concentrated on the superficial benefits of how my body looked, but the disciplined practice of athleticism and nutrition education proved itself as a healing agent for my mental well-being, including the internalized emotions that typically appeared in sharpness of mood swings, rage, and deep sadness.

Mesmerized by the people I'd see running down the street or on the treadmill for what seemed like hours without stopping, I became just as interested as I was irritated with the idea of running and decided I was going to figure it out. My pursuit began with intervals of running and walking a few minutes at a time until I was able to sustain a pace. I then pushed myself to go an even farther distance for prolonged amounts of time. With steady dedication day after day, what began as a challenge transformed me into a long-distance runner. Other than experiencing sore feet after putting in too many miles or wearing the wrong shoes without proper support, I had never experienced an athletic injury.

My fitness journey strengthened when I became exposed to high intensity interval training (HIIT). If you are familiar with HIIT-type exercises, then box jumps are likely familiar to you. When doing this exercise, athletes swing their arms and thrust their hips to jump from the ground to the top of a box. Box jumps work all of your leg and lower ab muscles. As you advance in fitness, the height of the box goes up to match your increase in strength, and an increase in box height is considered an achievement. The first time I was exposed to this exercise, I was coached to focus on proper form. With practice, I began to go higher and higher. During one particular workout session, after already completing an intense workout, I decided to practice my box jumps so that I could compete with some of the other athletes at being one of the best in the gym. The perfectionist mindset was strike one.

"First pride, then the crash—the bigger the ego, the harder the fall." — Proverbs 16:18 (MSG)

At first, I was shocked to find myself successfully landing with both feet on this wooden box more than half my height. I went for it again and again, discounting my body's fatigue, not realizing that my jumps were getting lower to the ground. That is where I messed up. As I leaped from the ground one last time, I fell short, and the edge of the wooden box, where my feet should have landed, seeped into my shins. It was awful. After experiencing that painful failed attempt and the ugly scars it left on my legs as a consequence, I vowed that I'd never do box jumps again.

A few years later, I began working with a new fitness coach who also focused on strength and HIIT training. Sure enough, there came a time that I was faced with performing box jumps to complete my workout session. I refused. I went right into my spiel, explaining what happened before, and pointed at the dotted scars on my shins that failed to fade. For some reason, my trainer was not fazed by my tantrum and, if anything, became more intense and persuasive in his rebuttal, stating that facing my fear was all the more reason I needed to try. To match my stubbornness, he offered a box no taller than a shoe box to complete my workout, reassuring me that he wouldn't let me fall. Finally, I went for it. Can you imagine a fit and able-bodied person screaming as if they were about to jump out of a plane and skydive for the first time, but in reality, they were jumping one foot off the ground, at best? I did. And I landed.

My physical body had healed from the injury I had experienced before, but my mind was wounded by the notion of facing that same obstacle and experiencing the same pain. My first injury impacted my mindset and what I could achieve as an athlete moving forward. In that moment, my trainer helped me see that my mind had deceived itself. Once my confidence began to grow in my present capabilities rather than memories from the past, I quickly found that I was a stronger athlete than before, I was able to clear higher box jumps than where I had fallen, and, subsequently, I had become stagnant.

When you sit in your memories and trauma, rehearsing injuries and negative outcomes over and again, reminding yourself of every painful thing that ever happened in your life, it doesn't matter how you look on the outside or what physical things you possess if you are tormented by pain. There is no achievement, degree, or accomplishment that will change your circumstance.

If you are not willing to rise again to face life's challenges, or release the weight of hurt with forgiveness, there is no purpose in chasing inanimate dreams. Sitting is choosing a position of ease and comfortability. Sitting in pain is an act of making yourself comfortable and complacent while resting in negative thoughts and attitudes.

I have lived with rage, mood swings, ruminating in my thoughts, and telling the same story over and over again of what happened to me and who did what to me, and it has tormented me and made me sick. If left unaddressed, toxic emotions will ruin your relationships, ruin your career, ruin your ability to love, and ruin your mind.

The process of survival will change you. It can make you hard and brittle—and, like scar tissue, deformed, less pliable to withstand being stretched—and without treatment, less capable of being moved. That is why you have to be intentional about living. You must practice being present and content, understanding that if you ignore the present long enough, you will lose the future. The past is a place of reference, not residence. You may have to see a therapist, take medicine, or even go away for a while to complete a treatment process to heal.

"The thief does not come except to steal, and to kill, and to destroy. I have come that they may have life, and that they may have it more abundantly." — John 10:10 (NKJV)

Whatever it takes, refuse to sit in isolation, remaining imprisoned to pain and living in the past. The present is an opportunity to reach new heights with new strength. Phenomenal faith is an exercise to move forward, not to sit in misery another day. It is the unmerited opportunity to turn the pages of life, understanding that with every new chapter, the story will change. Our bodies adjust to injury because we are created to survive. With having done all to stand, do not simply survive—transform.

Jessica C. Lumpkin,

Chapter 10
Story of Me

Hey there! My name is Ranika, I am a phenomenal woman, and I am also codependent. I bet you never thought you would see those words in a sentence together. *Duality, baby!* All jokes aside, I am living out one of my childhood dreams of writing. I am sitting at one of my favorite coffee shops in Tallahassee, with my latte ready, fingers flexed and ready to type. It is also a very important day for me… It is my CODA anniversary. Yes, you read that right: CODA, and it stands for Codependents Anonymous. Truthfully speaking, until I found that meeting, I never knew it existed or that I needed it. Like everyone else, I have gotten some nuggets of information from Instagram. I wouldn't recommend it to diagnose yourself, but there are some amazing people sharing their truths there.

The call for healing spreads far and wide, and I try to follow the little pocket of social media that promotes that. Anyways, I saw a post about a book called *Codependent No More* by Melody Beattie. As cocky as I sound, I got that book to prove that there were codependent people around me and that everyone else around me had the problems, which they may. But ultimately, I never saw mine, and if I did, they were minimal to me. Let me give you context on why that was rooted in arrogance and denial.

Let me paint the overall picture: I have my own mental diagnoses (depression, anxiety, PTSD, ADHD), unhealed trauma (emotional, verbal, and sexual abuse), and some other shit. And I had a chip on my shoulder, sitting high on my chair as if I was perfect. Oh, I thought none of these things affected me. Bruh! Self-righteousness is an uppity bitch! Why didn't anybody tell me? Some tried, and I wasn't listening. Defensiveness is something else. *Whew-wee!* I gave some of my more difficult traits names; it humanizes them for me, and I have more empathy in that way.

That book gave me a picture of behaviors, thoughts, and emotions I am all too familiar with having and operating from. Codependency can be in the form of caretaking, low self-worth, repression, obsession, controlling behavior, denial, dependency, poor communication, weak boundaries, lack of trust, anger, sex problems, and other extreme behaviors. Reading the examples out of each category made me pause and think, *Oh, shit. That's me. It was not pretty.*

When I turn the gaze inward, it is still not easy to see some of myself in those stories. Some of the positive codependency traits, like extremely responsible or overly passive, were things I knew I struggled with most of life. There is a questionnaire towards the back of the book. Let's just say I scored high enough to find one of those meetings they talked about in the book.

I had never been to any addiction meetings for myself before; I was always in a support role. This was a role I wore with pride because I was supportive of the person getting help, as Little Miss Fix It. You do not understand the dopamine high. It's the ego saying, "Look. You helped them!" *Translation: "You fixed them."*

Please do not get me wrong—I want to see everyone win and be the best versions of themselves, but not at the expense of others and avoiding my own work. Again, until three years ago, I had never fully turned the lens on myself and examined what was underneath. I could blame it on a host of things, like my astrological placements, upbringing, or traumatic experiences, but the truth is, I avoided responsibility and accountability in most areas of life because I did not have the proper tools. Although I've experienced some heavy shit from people that truly was not my fault, I used those experiences to excuse so many situations and defend some bullshit. We will get to that later.

Back to the lead-up to the meeting: I told my now-former wife that I was going, and she seemed supportive of it. It is humbling to refer to her as my former wife. I took that divorce as the ultimate failure, yet one of the biggest catalysts leading to the major shift in my life. If I wanted to change, I had to do it myself.

No one was coming to save me this time.

Here is the thing: Most addicts do not know they are addicts—or, they do know, and will try to deflect the light off of them before you can say something about their addiction. Most codependents do not know they are codependent until they are faced with the problem head-on. I would say death and divorce are pretty head-on. I think it is overlooked that addiction does not stop at alcohol, drugs, gambling, food, or any other outward vices. It can be as subtle as a particular train of thoughts and actions that lead to unhealthy relationships with self and others.

When I found the meeting, I initially thought I would do as I always do in new "healing" spaces: I would give it all of my attention and soak up all the information, go full throttle until the novelty wore off, and then move on to something else when it was too hard. I did it with my physical fitness journey. I declared, "Not this time!" I was determined, and I did not give up on either. After a few meetings, I realized it was one of the safest places I have been fortunate to be a part of. Everyone is there to address behaviors, patterns, and thoughts they are too ashamed of. I finally saw parts of myself I avoided or tried to hide. I faced the fact that I have struggled my whole life with close relationships; the closer the relationship, the more difficult it would be for me. Knowing that fact did not negate any conflict I had before. It did give me a chance to see I could choose differently. I could change myself and live a healthy and authentic life. It was an opportunity to build a relationship with myself without focusing on anyone else. Part of recovery is knowing that you will make amends with others, but the focus is a new, strong, and balanced foundation of self layered with acceptance, accountability, honesty, love, respect, and optimism—all things I had lost.

Last year was rough. Everything and everyone I placed my identity in was removed from my life. I never felt so alone and desperate for change. I did not think I would see the next year. I really did not want to see this year, but that one meeting truly changed my life. Acknowledging that today is my one-year CODA anniversary, I see last year as an opportunity from my Higher Power to connect with myself. I believe Spirit moves in unexplainable ways. I am grateful my meetings were temporarily replaced with Phenomenal Faith. It created a different kind of safe place to share my story.

A year ago, I went to my first meeting feeling a bit anxious. I walked in with my scrubs, Starbucks, Crocs, and nerves. It was like not knowing if you are going to do well on a test. The thing is, there is no test or grade; it is just you and God. I thought the people in the meeting couldn't relate to me or understand what I was going through. As I sat on the couch preparing for the meeting to start, I realized I had already judged these people, and I somewhat felt like they judged me, although they never did.

Newsflash: Another part of codependency is judgment and criticism, a direct reflection of the energy I gave myself. CODA is run the same way each time. I won't go into the structure, but I will say it is exactly like setting up your prayer room or altar—it has all the rituals to connect you with your higher power. Find spirituality in a CODA meeting—*yeah, right.*

When it came time for everyone to speak, people shared their stories of how codependency showed up in their lives. I realized that on a basic level, we all have some of the same trials and tribulations.

During a CODA meeting, there is a moment when anyone can share a burning desire; the floor is yours with no judgment and no interruption. A burning desire to share actually came over me. So, I shared where I was in life, replaying what I could recall. Life was happening to me, and I was not stable at all. I did not see light, it was really dark, and my normal operating system of "Fake it till you make it" kicked in. A good part of 2021 was spent on autopilot, and I knew I needed some serious help. There was so much going on in my life. I had no idea where to go or what to do.

The first meeting found me about two weeks or so post-breakup. I do not think the magnitude of my marriage ending hit me when I attended the first meeting. I casually said it out loud, but connecting with what it meant took a few more meetings.

I distinctly remember checking out. I felt so numb inside, like my spirit and flesh were disconnected. I felt like a failure. I did not feel full or connected, but I did lean into my spiritual practices harder—something had to give, and soon. I grabbed crystals, tarot cards, astrology apps, books, journals, self-help podcasts—you name it, I grabbed it. I prayed and begged God, the Universe, ancestors, anyone who could listen, to help me out. These are all tools I'd used before, but this time was different. There was a desperation I had only met a few times in my life. It was darker, though, like seeing light through the tiniest cracks, clinging more to the idea of light than actually seeing it. This darkness could not stay because it was somehow taking over more and more, like a slow ooze. There is no doubt I was in a depressive episode, so much so that I was contemplating living a bicoastal lifestyle in Tallahassee and Los Angeles with no plan, no financial stability, nothing—just a possible escape.

In the few months leading up to the first meeting, life flew by me at a lightning speed. I wanted to feel something other than agony.

Damn it! I'm out of coffee. Hold on. I will be right back with some more thoughts and reflections.

Bam! I am back. I just reread the initial version of this chapter, which sounded more like a research paper than a story of who I am. The fact is, my story and who I am are still sometimes a mystery to me. Every day, I am unpacking the old and gaining something new. What I can tell you is that I have struggled in all areas and with the closest people in my life. One thing about codependent people: We will contort ourselves in and out of situations until we can't anymore. For the better part of my early life, I was hell-bent on blending in and contorting myself to fit the status quo, but I have always been different. I have always stood out, and I experienced some of the most profound moments of my life when I did just that—stood the fuck out. I never felt like I fully fit in with family, friends, or in work spaces; some of it was self-imposed. Let me start off by saying that this story isn't about one particular part of or event in my life. It is how I got to this coffee shop on this day, writing these words.

I was listening to this podcast called *Affirmations for Black Girls,* and the host did a series on childhood trauma. There are so, *so* many things I thought were normal that could be considered direct and indirect traumas. She listed quite a few, and they resonated with me. I sat with what my response was to each of them. I decided that when I found the answers, I would put them here. I thought long and hard about if I would write about my childhood sexual trauma specifically in this chapter, but I decided not to because my purpose is sharing who and where I am now. I allowed that trauma to color a lot of my life experiences, so I now choose to acknowledge it and leave it where it is: in my past.

I wondered why it was so hard for me to write during these last couple of weeks. I just couldn't do it. And now, we're in it, at the end of this journey. Honestly, a part of it is that I am currently on the tail end of another high-functioning depressive episode. My mind would have me believe that my words aren't important, but I know that is a lie.

This opportunity to write came at a pivotal time in my journey. It is something I have always wanted to do. I tried to start a blog a few years ago, but I was not ready to be honest with myself. I am in one of the biggest transitions of my life. I used to identify as a perfectionistic procrastinator or a procrastinating perfectionist—either way, they contradict each other a lot in my life. I learned from CODA that both are rooted in self-worth and confidence. My life has often mirrored whoever is leading that day. I have always had that struggle between polar opposites, internally and externally. Starting over in life for me brings out the extremes. For instance, the dreamer in me romanticized the idea of writing a chapter in this book, so I jumped on it. I have started the same introduction a million different ways; I have deleted so many incomplete thoughts. Two things about me: (1) I love change, and (2) I hate discomfort. It's probably why I tend to get to a cushy place in my healing journey and ride it out. I also hate starting over and not knowing things, yet I know that every time I have felt discomfort thus far, it sparked a significant change that led to a new life.

I've had high-functioning depression for a long time. I did

not have the vocabulary or knowledge to understand what that means until recently. When I struggled with thoughts of self-harm, I kept to myself out of fear of judgment. "You cannot heal what you do not reveal." It took at least four years of therapy to talk about my childhood with honesty, and not in a "Do not tell them what I said" way. There was the fear that I was betraying my family by talking about my experience, or that the therapist would call them and tell them. It seems childish, but those were real thoughts and fears of mine. There is also the fact that it took years to accept that some of my childhood was not normal; this also plays a part in my current life.

I do not think I had a horrible childhood, but I do think I missed some of my childhood because I moved on autopilot. I was too busy playing a role I thought I had to play. I isolated myself from the world because I did not want the secret shame or pain to show. I had a darkness growing inside of me, and it ran the show. I harbored secrets with so much shame around them.

But in this phase of life, I want to be a part of as many safe circles and communities as I can because it gives me light in my darker times. I can also shine my light so others know they aren't alone. Some of the thoughts shared here are what I feel in my darker times; it's raw, it's honest, and it is some of what I have battled my whole life.

High-functioning depressive people do not function out of joy. It is in response to some type of triggered emotion or thought. It is survival mode.

There are so many points in my life when I literally wanted to fall apart. I did not want to exist. Last year, I was physically at my brother's funeral, but mentally, I was so far gone. I wanted something strong to numb myself—maybe do *more* than numb—but thank God that "something" never came.

When I slowed my mind down, I said the following:

Fuck that. Fuck that. It is okay to break the fuck down. It is okay to scream. It is okay to be fucking angry with the world right now because it's some fucking bullshit.

I prayed to be where my brother was. I prayed to be where my uncle was, where my grandparents were, where my cousins were, where my family was.

I prayed that prayer. Thank God. Thank God that Spirit did not listen to me, because I would not be here.

When I get up in the morning, I thank God that I did not go with creating a plan because I get to see another day. But then, I look at my altar, I see my brother, and I realize my brother does not have any more days. *He never came back.* I have so much shit I want to tell him, to show him, to express to him how much I love him. That was the one person I knew in this life who never judged me. He never made me feel unworthy, unheard, unseen, or unvalued, ever. If you want to look at unconditional love, it's my brother, and I miss him, and I don't fully understand this life without him. At first, I thought I could take away my pain, but that is not realistic for anyone grieving a loved one who has passed on. You can try to run or hide from the grief for a bit. That finally stopped working, and CODA entered my life. Again, it was a gift from Heaven, but I was back to facing the thoughts that paralyze me.

I didn't break down because I've allowed myself to believe that the people around me are not used to me breaking down, and I feared they can't fucking handle it. It's a response I have had since childhood; thankfully, it is not following me into the next phase of my life. I dropped that belief. It is heavy to carry grief without support. There's a resurgence of peace. And we can tell people, "You just gotta get through the darkness," but everybody's darkness is different. And somehow, some way, I have made it through mine—at least, at this point in my life. But I'm lucky I'm beating the fucking odds, 'cause there are a lot of people who have walked in similar shoes as me—and I mean *similar*—and they're not here to tell their stories. I think the twelve steps really helped me widen that crack so that more light could shine through. I had no choice other than leaning deeply into them. Of all the things I have shared, the twelve steps put things into context and gave me some kind of navigation out of the darkness.

Step 1: We admitted we were powerless over others—that our lives had become unmanageable. (I could not bring my brother or uncle back, and I could not undo the damage in my marriage. I can't make anyone be or do anything. It is arrogant to try to be in control of someone else's healing.)

Step 2: We came to believe that a power greater than ourselves could restore us to sanity. (I had believed what I felt was temporary and I would be able to move on.)

Step 3: We made a decision to turn our will and our lives over to the care of God as we understood God. (As a control freak, surrendering to God was hard, and it cracked my ego in the best of ways.)

Step 4: We made a searching and fearless moral inventory of ourselves. (I am still working on this. It's a continuous process of learning and unlearning.)

Step 5: We admitted to God, to ourselves, and to another human being the exact nature of our wrongs. (Whew! Again, it was a humbling experience being alone and facing myself. I have to fess up to things every day and be forgiven.)

These steps really were interchangeable for the first few months. I threw pity and martyr parties, all the while still having ideations come through, but the difference was that the impulse to do anything was fading. People need to stop demonizing suicidal thoughts and stop telling people that they are weak when they have suicidal thoughts or ideations, because they're not. They're fucking hurting. Recognizing that I had these exact sets of thoughts before and I made it through, I started to shift the negatives into positives. I have attempted two times and thought really hard on the third.

The first time I tried to kill myself, I was sixteen. I took one of either my brother's or my dad's, belts. And I said, *fuck it.* So, I tied it onto the shower and I said, *Well, this is—this is it.* I put it around my neck, and I went to jump, and I just couldn't do it.

The summer before my senior year of high school, my

family and I took a road trip to Memphis, Tennessee. I fell in love with seeing all the new places, faces, and experiences as the desire to see more grew. At some point towards the end of the trip, everything went left. For the life of me, I cannot remember what us kids argued about, but it led to fighting the whole way back. I really didn't care because all the fights sounded the same and I had my own issues to worry about. Either I was going to end my life, or I was going to get as far away from it as possible. A thought was clear: *Come hell or high water, I am leaving as soon as I graduate high school.*

During that period of time, I really felt lost and alone. The later part of my teen years, I masked how I felt so well that I didn't know how I truly felt. To combat those feelings, I dug deep into my senior year experience. I was vice president of the Black Student Union, senator of the drama club, and manager of the girl's basketball team, and I was also a member of the video production club and the yearbook and journalism club. I kept myself busy till it was time to leave. Then, two months after high school, I was off to the Army.

Part of this journey was a struggle because I know I need to give context of what was happening in my life and why I wanted to kill myself. I know that once I write these words, there is no turning back. When I was fifteen, I experienced sexual abuse from a close family member. I'm choosing not to give specific details because I don't need to share them to tell you they impacted my life and my view of the world. I developed so much shame and guilt that I carried well into my adulthood. I learned to trust people to a certain extent, including myself. Do you know how crazy it is not to trust yourself? I am unlearning so many things from unpacking these experiences. I spent years running from them and trying to outwork them with the military, until I started running from that, too.

During my period of service, I lived two different lives and only invested in my home life via phone calls and pop-up visits once or twice a year. When I suppressed my feelings, I found ways to channel that energy into a new professional achievement or personal possession. I assumed that I was correctly processing my experiences and not letting things get to me because feelings were useless. The Army reinforced the belief that thinking logically was the appropriate way to deal with any situation that occurred. It wasn't until marriage that the two perspectives collided, and an internal war erupted inside of me. I will never forget my first day out of the Army.

Deep down, I knew my time in the service was coming to an end, but I wanted to leave on my terms. I did not want my career ripped away from me. When I left the Army, it affected me more than anyone knows. Coming home represented all the fears of failure I had, and it also meant I could no longer run from my problems. All the harmful antics were destroying me and the world around me. I was heavier in every sense of the word, and I wore depression like a signature Bath and Body Works scent. I was happy to spend time reconnecting with my family, but I also felt like a fraud.

Game time, Nikki! Like every family, everyone has roles, and my role is to be the rational and logical thinker—the fixer, if you will. But was this really my role, or was it something I learned to do? To feel seen or valued—better yet, included—I learned the duties of my role after my grandma passed, and I took it harder than I ever showed. Three months into moving back home, my grandfather died. It shook everyone up, but it also meant that someone had to take care of his affairs. This was the catalyst for my second suicide attempt. I remember asking someone for some pain meds, knowing they contradicted the medication I was on. I never took them, though. I needed an outlet, and I needed one fast.

I was in my late twenties. I figured college would be a nice distraction from these things called feelings. One of the biggest things I learned when going to college was the importance of understanding African-American psychology and sociology. I was able to find myself. I was able to understand the psychology of what it's like to be a Black woman in particular, and I was able to just experience Blackness. We are really hard on ourselves when we don't achieve perfection or excellence, and psychologically, after generations and generations, that takes a toll on us. We feel like we have to be these pristine beings because it's instilled in his country that being Black, we already are viewed a particular way, and we don't want to be a stereotype. It leads to us being really hard on ourselves and our communities. And I think if we created and allowed spaces for each of us to be our individual selves, if we created spaces where we didn't have to carry loads by ourselves, particularly Black women, I do believe that a lot of the ideations, the thoughts, and the actions regarding suicidal behavior would see a change.

I really think that the narrative of the strong Black woman has hindered us a lot because there's an expectation to be strong, and that expectation has been here for generations. And I'm only thirty-six, but watching the generations underneath me has been so enlightening because they're able to articulate these things. They know when they're highly depressive. They know these things about themselves, which allows them to navigate the world differently, instead of finding out later and then having to abruptly change the way they navigate their lives. I'm happy to have found out these things about myself. When I found out about 'em, my path changed.

I never knew how to connect with Spirit authentically, but over the last few years, I have done so. Whether it was discovering crystals, tarot, sermons, CODA, or the gym, each continues to bring beautiful healing energies to my life. I have learned about myself, and I couldn't be prouder of the woman I am today. I could not be more thankful for the life that I live today. I could not be more grateful for the individuals—past, present, and future—in my life.

Step 6: We were entirely ready to have God remove all these defects of character. (It is a lonely journey, keeping people at bay and needing to be right instead of heard.)

Step 7: We humbly asked God to remove our shortcomings. (Please help me let go of anything that no longer serves me or use a protective measure against trauma.)

Step 8: We each made a list of all persons we had harmed, and became willing to make amends to them all. (I am still working on this one. I think it's a lifetime of work. I am learning how to make space for others' experiences and owning my parts in relationships.)

Step 9: We made direct amends to such people wherever possible, except when to do so would injure them or others.

Step 10: We continued to take personal inventory, and when we were wrong, we promptly admitted it. (I have anxious and avoidant attachment styles, so this prompt admission is still a work in process.)

Step 11: We sought, through prayer and meditation, to improve our conscious contact with God as we understood God, praying only for knowledge of God's will for us and the power to carry that out.

Step 12: Having had a spiritual awakening as the result of these steps, we tried to carry this message to other codependents and practice these principles in all our affairs.

I have gotten in the habit of reading the CODA moments of the day before my feet touch the ground each morning. This morning's CODA meditative moment says, "In this moment, I live for today. I am a child of God. This way of thinking hasn't always been easy for me. I have to remind myself to live in the moment. I set boundaries on the 'committee in my head.' I stop obsessing over, 'What if?,' 'I can't,' or 'I shouldn't.' When I am open to my Higher Power's will, my mind becomes free of the old tapes. I learn new messages. When I am relaxed and calm, I find the joy of living in peace, the meaning of true serenity in my mind, body, and spirit. I don't fret about tomorrow. I live for today."

This last year taught me that really working these steps will change a person's life. Every day is a different step. Sometimes, there isn't an order to them; they just need to be applied. I feel like the first six steps are the work that needs to be done, and the last six are the rewards for hard work. Sometimes, it can save relationships, and other times, just give the closure needed to move on. Going to the meetings reminds me of church. I do not always go, but every time I step across the threshold, there is a divine message waiting for me.

Thank you. I could not be more honored to write these words. I could not be more optimistic about the future. Maybe part of my journey is maintaining those thoughts and allowing myself the necessary space to process them, knowing that they are just that—thoughts—and that they will pass.

I have strength. I have resilience. Most of all, I have connections. I have community. I have love. I have joy. I have peace. I have excitement. *I have me.* I don't have to do this thing called life alone or perfectly, and it is fuller. Do you know how different it has been since giving up perfection and allowing myself grace to mess up and receive support?

If anything, coming out of last year, I learned to live for myself, be in love with myself, and do all the things that genuinely please me, and just be really grateful for life. I might fail again, or have my heart broken, I don't know. But endings happen, and I will always be with me. Honestly, it's the first time in my life when being alone feels like a blessing and gift instead of a curse. Making decisions from this perspective has given me a new level of self-confidence.

I want to be here for me. I know what the darkest part of night is for me. And *I made it.* I made it through. That's why I'm grateful. I'm grateful for every tool. I am grateful for every prayer, for every meditation, for every journal, for every cry, for every scream, for every long ass drive, for every blunt (yes, I said that), for every shot, for every single thing that has led me to the place that I am in right now. My life was divinely ordered.

I'm living the life I dreamed of—maybe not in the exact way I imagined it, but I always wanted to find myself, and I did. I always wanted to love myself, and I do. I always wanted to have my dream career, and now, I have it. I always wanted to be at peace with myself; namaste, Ranika.

I always wanted to build a solid connection with my Higher Power. I always wanted to be proud of who I am and where I come from. And I am.

A show I enjoy, *P-Valley*, just ended. One of my favorite lines from the show is that of the Lil Murder: "May the light find you in the darkest of shadows." There were significant lessons in the dark I had to experience. It is kind of like driving on the long stretch of I-10, from Santa Monica to Jacksonville; there are long stretches of highway where there is night, just following the GPS all the way through. Something I love to think about is no matter how dark that drive gets, there's a bright beach on either side. I have taken that journey three times, each with one lesson.

So, whatever I-10 looks like in your life, you can get to the other side of it. Just keep driving through. The other day, I was pulling tarot cards, and they said that I should use my authentic voice. I pulled other ones, and they said, "Don't let fear stop you." I pulled a few other ones, too. I won't let fear stop me because I know fear is one of those voices talking. *That means me no good.* I know that fear comes from a lack of comfort due to a lot of changes and the unknown. Nothing in this life is known, and there is a freedom in that. One of my clients said she had happiness for a really long time with her husband of fifty-two years. Since she is now alone, she wants to know peace. I asked her why she doesn't find happiness in her peace. Everything, and I do mean everything, comes from within first. In the words of Beyoncé on "VIRGO'S GROOVE," "A psychic hit me, told me we got shit to do. We ain't got time like we used to, but we still shine like we used to, and we still grind like we used to, and we cut ties when we need to."

Well, it's time to go. One, I ran out of coffee, and two, I gotta pee. Again, if you're going to read my words, you're going to get my thoughts as they come.

Ranika Rashawn

Chapter 11

I Am Tomi

There's a way to reconstruct just about every part of the body. When a body part breaks or is no longer functioning properly, there are doctors that specialize in specific practices and experts that can get you back on track. A podiatrist can perform an Achilles tendon repair on the foot. A cardiologist can examine and treat your heart. A pulmonologist can resolve your respiratory issues. An orthopedist can treat acute and chronic knee pain. Even for the minor occurrences, like a broken nail, a nail technician can fix your nail so that it is just as beautiful as your other nails. And God's gift to us all, a beautician, can make you look like a million bucks on a bad hair day! But when your soul is broken, who do you go to for soul repair?

I found myself pondering that question when I was reflecting on the events from climbing the first mountain of my life that led me to seek out soul repair. At times, I felt depleted, discouraged, and even a little depressed. I did not feel as though I was enough at times in my adolescent and adult years, and as a result of it, I became a people-pleaser.

My Aunt Moji gave me the name Tomi. My first thought was, *Why would she give me a boy name?* I was such a girly child, and the thought of letting my friends know I am "Tomi" was not happening. Later in my adult years, I learned more about my Nigerian culture, and the name "Tomi" means "enough." The name is short for Oluwatomi, which is of Nigerian origin, meaning "God is enough." My paternal family is from a Yoruba lineage in Nigeria. When my Aunt Moji gifted me with my name, she knew it would be a gentle reminder I would one day need to restore my soul.

I am Tomi.

We all enter this world alone, and we will leave the same way. What is important is how you value yourself while you are here. As my father would say, "Everyone has their own life to live." I took this as him allowing me to live my life as I saw fit with the glory of God. I could appreciate my father releasing control of my life and setting me free to win and make mistakes in life. Can you imagine what life would be like today if Dr. Martin Luther King's dad told him to stop speaking love to the people because he was fearful of losing his son? This is why we learn to listen to God as the engineer of our lives and allow Him to lead us to a purpose-driven life.

I view life as a moving train to self-discovery and finding one's purpose. Self-discovery will help you value your uniqueness and self-worth. The sooner you can discover your true self as the conductor of the train that is your life, you will know exactly whose admission ticket you should accept or not. Just know there will be people to charm their way onto your train to throw you off course. As the conductor, you are responsible for managing the activities and people on your train, including yourself. Self-discovery will give you discernment to take notice of charming and charismatic people.

Unfortunately, I was not aware of how charming people could use manipulative techniques and behaviors to get what they wanted from me. This would be a recurring problem in my life. I was a people-pleaser, and I realized that by always telling people "yes," I was telling myself "no": No, my needs do not have to be met. No, what they are asking me is more important than what I have going on at the moment. No, I can't let them down, so I will drop everything for them. People-pleasing was threaded in the fabric of my heart. Naturally, I am a helper, and I love helping my family and friends. I thought I was being a kind and loving person by making people happy.

There is a difference between being a kind person and being a people-pleaser. I believe the need to help comes from the adversities I faced over time. There are people who will board your life train for a reason, a season, or a lifetime. The key is to appreciate each reason or season if a person decides to depart your train. Each person who departs leaves a little token of life lessons behind. Many of these lessons were designed to motivate you, elevate you, and uplift your soul. Some lessons were designed to delay or redirect your journey. What is important is that you learn from each lesson so you do not have to face the same test over and over again in life.

As a young single parent, I faced many adversities. I learned my life lessons from some, and I am continuing to learn from others. I quickly learned one of the most valuable lessons of being a single parent: You do not have time to cry over the betrayals and the abandonment you will face. There were so many people I expected to say yes, and they consistently told me no in the worst ways. Some dropped the phone, yelled, lied, or did not answer. To make matters worse, there were people who I thought had my best interests at heart, but, in reality, they bet on me losing in life or did not want to be bothered with my issues as a young single parent that could make smart decisions. I was told I would not graduate high school, attend college, or become a teacher. But look at me now!

The worst betrayal was when they made me feel like I did not have the capacity to be a good mother. Many of these occurrences made me think that I was not good enough, smart enough, or ready enough to make it in life. I began to hear my dream blockers say, "You should drop out of school, go to work, and raise your child." I managed to suppress all of my feelings of despair and became determined. I had to suck it up and move on in life because life was not just about me anymore. I knew every moment I spent crying and complaining over the fact that I was a struggling teen parent living on the couch of a friend was a big distraction. My reality said I would not make it, but my faith instilled in me said, "I can do all things through Christ who strengthens me" (Philippians 4:13).

My life mantra is, "The impossible is always possible." In order to overcome life's obstacles and adversities, I had to be real with who I am, become numb to the pain of my current situation, and press through to create a better lifestyle for me and my child. I wanted only one thing: I wanted my child to be SMART. I knew that in order to do so, as her mother, I had to become SMART. So, I decided to change my mindset and way of living by changing our environment. We left sweet home Alabama.

I didn't have time to waste, and I needed to get started on a journey towards a better life by relocating to live with my father in a different state. We were not seeing eye to eye at the time. He was still getting over the hurt that his child had a child, but he welcomed us into his home in Sandy Springs, Georgia.

I believe many factors led to me being a people-pleaser as a single parent striving to survive. For instance, I experienced poor self-esteem issues as a new resident in a big city as I sought acceptance at work, school, and home. I did not have any friends at the time, and it took time to adjust to the new city and culture.

In addition, I would be cautious as a single parent, which involved me helping another person or single parent as a result of me needing help later. For example, I often *came to the rescue* of many single parents and did not seek anything in return but loyalty. As a result, I did not need as much support as I gave out, but I connected with many phenomenal women who were hands up in my life. I learned to strengthen my God-given gifts by surrounding myself with women with strong faith and parenting skills.

As a new African-American college student and worker, I did not feel educated enough. I was aware that I had academic challenges due to being raised in a struggling single-parent home and attending low-performing schools the majority of my childhood. I also grew up hearing, *"As a Black woman, you have to work twice as hard."* The feeling of not being enough was deep-rooted.

Lastly, I believe my humble past experiences provoked me to treat people how I wanted to be treated. There were many times when I felt betrayed by loved ones who dropped the ball in my life. I was disappointed by the many people who failed to take action or do something they were supposed to, or who deliberately added extra weight to my life. My kindness was often taken for a weakness as a strong, empathetic woman, especially by narcissists, energy vampires, and controllers. I call these types of people dream blockers. They come to steal, kill, or destroy.

If you pay close attention, dream blockers really do not offer anything of value to you, although they require so much of your energy, time, or money. Dream blockers will slow you down with their charming techniques. Their main objective is to break your soul; some of them may not be aware of the negative energy they are giving off. They want you to stop what you are doing to please and serve them, no matter what it may cost you in life. They don't care. Periodt.

Every journey comes with the right people and the wrong people. The right people will push you to move forward, and the wrong people will get in your way, slow you down or stop you. As a single parent, you will encounter some form of betrayal until you connect with the right people on your journey. My journey at the time was becoming a SMART mom. Life did not get better for me until I connected with other strong, smart single parents. They understood me, inspired me, and pushed me right along on my single parent journey.

No matter what, I made it a point to be good to my support group of single parents, and I never dropped the ball on them. If I committed to something, I did it, and I did not want them to experience the betrayal I had endured in the past—for example, my daughter's father refusing to be a full-time parent, us having to live with others as a result of my mother being a surviving single parent, and my father's lack of concern for me during the times I needed him most due to his disapproval of me becoming an unwed teen mom or not.

Ironically, as an adult, my motivation to help others became a form of altruism. I became a person who genuinely wanted to ensure that other people had the help they needed. I accepted the life purpose of supporting single parents, children, education, and community. I felt valued, and I gained happiness by helping others become unstuck to survive as single parents.

My everyday life was filled with small acts of altruism, such as educating children, teaching survival skills to single parents, supporting women in domestic violence situations, giving money to people in need, feeding the hungry, helping people in housing transitions, building individuals' career readiness needs, showing people how to make money on the side, and helping people be mobile by teaching them to drive.

I even went as far as financing cars for people with my savings. This all happened in my twenties, and I was on fire! It makes me wonder what is possible in my forties. I found joy in helping people, even if it meant depleting my time and energy. I shared survival skills and resources to help others without the expectations of rewards. I took my purpose everywhere I went: to work, church, school, the doctor's office, and even parties. Encouraging people on my everyday walk in life became my purpose. I learned from one of the best Mary Kay Directors that you sell your Mary Kay products everywhere you go. I did the same with my purpose for supporting single families. As a result of seeing so many people's lives change, I continued for years. I developed a love for helping others, even though my help was limited.

Depleted

The problem with pleasing people is that not only did I put the needs of others before my own, but when the time came for me to lean on others, they did not reciprocate the help. It was not until I turned forty that my single parent life had ended. The moment I had been waiting for my entire life was happening. My child was not only graduating college—she had obtained true love and a well-paying job, too. I was beyond feeling blessed because my child was now a successful, strong Black woman. She had earned a job working with predominantly older white males. I felt so honored to have raised a daughter who broke the glass ceiling in the construction field. As a project manager for a top homebuilding company, where she built eleven homes in one year. She was skilled and equipped to live the life of her dreams on her own with my teaching. I have given her the gifts of living and financially supporting herself. I officially raised a "badass" as

232

a woman.

I was overwhelmed with joy, but in pain at the same time. I was at the peak of my first mountain, but I held a numb feeling in my heart again. I had accomplished everything I'd set out to obtain, but I was unsatisfied. I was not completely happy with the fact that I graduated college; became a teacher, business owner, community leader, and homeowner; and raised a SMART child.

I was barely able to hold it together, and felt like I had no more fight in me. Something was wrong. The day of my daughter's graduation brunch, I had just received the news that a close relative had passed away. I had been up the entire night on the phone with a friend from overseas who helped me, ensuring that everything was right for my daughter's brunch. I took a minute to experience my grief, but I didn't have the time or energy to process the loss. I had to push forward and show up happy for my daughter. I looked around the room, appreciative of the many loved ones who showed up to celebrate my child, but I allowed myself to be saddened by the family and friends who expressed no interest in showing up. Now, many people could not show up for a multitude of reasons, but there were people who continued to show a disinterest in the major milestones of our lives. How I felt about my daughter's big day was no secret.

In 2014, I became open with our mother-daughter relationship online. So many people inboxed me over the years and thanked me for sharing our mother-daughter love. They would share how much they were inspired by our relationship. This made me feel proud of my purpose. However, what depleted me is when we sent graduation invitations to family and very close friends, who ignored the invitation from my daughter, and they did not bother to congratulate her online, by text, or in person. I thought, *What have we done?' It is amazing how silence can speak louder than words. I asked myself, Why would this happen, when I've gone out of my way to celebrate their milestones?* It began to eat me up inside, and I was tired of this feeling.

I was hurt, and let's just say, some people do not fail to disappoint. They have a way of keeping the same energy. It was important to see this before moving on to my life's second mountain. On my drive home from attending my close relative's funeral and feeling deleted from the week, I became lost in my thoughts and pain. I traveled to a different state by mistake. I discovered I was alone on the mountainside of Chattanooga, Tennessee. After getting lost in Tennessee, I finally understood the saying, "Not everyone can come with you on your journey." It was a hard pill to swallow, but I've been down this road before with people. This was the final straw. Something had to change. I had to change, and I realized that I needed to unplug from distractions and plug into my source.

I cried. Then, I cried out to God: "I need You and only You. God, change the way that I show up for others, and more importantly, God, change how I show up for myself." For the degree of repair that my soul needed, I was going to need more than a prayer and a gospel song. I needed to restore my relationship with God.

Discouraged

In 2017, California congresswoman Maxine Waters stated that she was "reclaiming her time" during a U.S. House Committee on Financial Services hearing. Congressman Waters asked specific questions to Treasury Secretary Steven Mnuchin, and she wanted him to answer directly and precisely so as to not eat up their hearing time. When he began to deflect, her response was, "I'm reclaiming my time," and the internet erupted! There were songs and memes everywhere; it became a catchphrase. It also became one of my personal mantras. But when I heard the catchphrase from a good friend who was exhausted from the expectation of being there for everyone and had decided she was reclaiming her time for her personal wellness, I could relate. After being strong in every aspect of my life as someone's child, sister, mother, aunt, co-worker, and the list goes on, it hit home that this is how I was feeling, as well. I wanted to obtain the freedom I was seeking after carrying others' weight for so long. I was done and ready to live life on my own terms and not for others anymore. I too was reclaiming my time and ready to "be free" in 2023!

In 2022, I experienced some serious health challenges as a hard-working forty-year-old woman. As a result, I had two surgeries, and oddly enough, I was shocked by the lack of concern shown by people I had placed on the frontline in my life. It's understood that people are wrapped up in their own concerns, families, and busy lives, and that they need rest. I am never a needy person. In a time of distress, you want to know that your close circle of people care about your well-being enough to offer emotional support. The first surgery was for the removal of fibroids that I'd suffered with for an entire year, but the aftermath was the worst. I experienced extreme pain over the course of two weeks.

I was grateful to raise a beautiful daughter who reciprocated the love I shared. It was a proud moment to see my daughter doing an excellent job caring for me at her home. She did everything right. She took me to my doctor appointments, consulted with the doctor, picked up my prescriptions, prepared healthy food options for me, and distributed my medications. Although I was only overdosed once, I was still happy to see the care and thoughtfulness my child possessed. I immediately felt blessed before sleeping for hours from the extra pain medicine she gave me.

I appreciated the fact that my daughter did a great job, and I did not want to take up too much of her space and time. I insisted on taking care of myself by returning home alone when I thought I felt well enough to be on my own. That was the biggest mistake I could have ever made. After a few nights of tossing and turning in excruciating pain on my living room floor, I gave in and reached out to a couple of people for help. It had been five days without making a bowel movement. I was not aware that several days without a bowel movement could be a serious matter, so I proceeded to reach out to close family and friends.

Unfortunately, I contacted the same family and friends who had disappointed me in the past, and their lack of interest in my health was undeniable. They managed to keep the same energy of not giving a damn. I asked for simple things, like water, Tylenol, and feminine products, and I wasn't surprised by the lack of compassion in a family member's voice when they asked why they should get those things for me and suggested that I use services like Instacart and Amazon for my needs. And honestly, I would have done so, but I was not familiar with the online services. I was disappointed with myself more than anything for continuing to entertain relationships that were one-sided. It did not matter that I'd spent years bending over backwards for them.

They were saying "no" to me once again, and I had said "yes" countlessly. This moment reminded me yet again of the countless times they denied me help as a single parent. I quickly reverted back to being a strong woman and enduring the pain alone on the floor. The pain had increased and traveled up my back. My daughter had already done so much, and I did not want to bother her. I was still processing the fact that I needed care from my daughter at such a young age and did not want to be a burden. God's grace is always perfect. When I accepted that I was going to embrace the pain alone, I began receiving an abundance of emotional support from my school parents, neighbors, and a friend. I thought, God does not disappoint. He is always there when you need Him the most. I remembered that my great- grandmother, Mary, would always say, "Be mindful of how you treat people because you never know who is going to give you your last drink of water."

A caring friend had shown up in my life at the right time. Our lives were parallel; she was a strong woman, single mom, educator, and businesswoman. She was the person in my life that I had been for so many other people. She understood me. However, it was difficult for me to receive love in the beginning because I didn't want to feel vulnerable. I had been a strong woman for years, and I did not want to be a burden on anyone. She insisted on coming over to my home to purchase groceries, prepare meals, and nurse me without any expectations or rewards. Although I had been hurt by people who chose not to reciprocate my love, I was grateful for the love I received from my child, loved ones, neighbors, and school parents. More than anything, I was thankful and happy to finally poop!

The second surgery was for a pulmonary embolism, which also triggered my asthma. I had always heard that a blood clot could be deadly, and I never imagined it happening to me so young. The response from the friends and family members I reached out to was the dealbreaker for me.

Many of them expressed concerns for my health and wanted to come see me. A couple of them went the extra mile to ensure that I was okay. Due to the circumstances, I did not want to be stressed with an overwhelming number of people in the hospital. I assured loved ones who reached out with genuine concern or to offer prayer and moral support that I was stable so I could rest to heal. Many of their initial reactions were enough for me; I knew they were genuinely concerned about my health. I have never been a needy person, but I do like to know that my life is valued by the people I cherish the most. However, I found it bizarre that the "friends" who I had dropped everything to be there for when they were sick, hungry, grieving, or just in need of a friend did not reciprocate that love when I needed to feel it the most. I was flabbergasted and hurt by shady responses from the friends who I showed up and overexerted myself for in the past. I began to feel broken until I thought, Peter betrayed Jesus, so who am I?

The reasons for them not being able to visit or help me varied: they were working, they had plans to go to the mall, they were attending a birthday party, etc. Other friends simply ignored me entirely and didn't say a word. Some sent vague texts, and I never heard from them again. I was like, "Damn!" A hospital visit didn't mean anything to them. After arriving at the emergency room, I remember my daughter's boyfriend rushing to the hospital because he was worried about my well-being, which makes him a keeper—especially when he decided to bring us food from Waffle House.

Although we were calm about the situation, his actions of concern were genuine, and I will cherish that moment forever. Everything was normal until a nurse called me to the back. I realized my situation was critical when I needed two doctors, a cardiologist, and a pulmonologist. Everything became fuzzy and rushed. Moments later, I was getting prepped to be transported to a second hospital by ambulance for surgery. Although I was nervous, I felt safe because the doctors were knowledgeable and kind. Shortly afterwards, a kind lady with an autism support-themed cap transferred me, holding on to my bag of items and Waffle House breakfast, from room 40 to room 24. My initial thoughts were that the numbers on my room doors were the same as my age and my daughter's age. However, after several nurses and doctors entered the room to care for me, one phone call greatly concerned me.

My daughter called to check on me, and I began to break because I could tell she had been crying. I thank God for sending her boyfriend to comfort her. Although I can be a private person, we needed him. I couldn't imagine her being alone while her mother was in such terrible condition. At this point, I had to be strong and endure whatever I was going through to return to my child and loved ones. I knew I could not allow my daughter to hear me upset, so I suppressed my emotions with jokes and laughter to hold it together if she called again.

While in the emergency room, I received a strange visit from hospital personnel asking if I had a living will. Of course, I responded with a bizarre look to the question because my critical state still did not register until that point. Then, my phenomenal faith kicked into overdrive. With the nurse's permission, I quickly gulfed down the Waffle House meal from my daughter's boyfriend and became extremely serious about taking on this storm.

Ignorance is bliss. If not for my ignorance, I probably would have panicked, and matters could have worsened. Unfortunately, I had no time for that. I had to prepare to fight and get back to my child, family, and friends. I could not focus on the problem of having blood clots in both of my lungs. The X-ray clearly showed multiple pulmonary emboli, and a person's heart becomes strained when it is overworked by the lack of blood flow to the muscle, causing chest pain, shortness of breath, dizziness, and weird ocean sounds to the ears. My lungs were so full of blood clots that the doctor had to extract them. I was sedated with medications, but I could hear and see everything as I was in and out of sleep. The anxiety came when I decided to watch, on the large screen, the pulmonologist and cardiologist enter my lungs to remove the clots. I attempted to force myself to sleep to keep myself from panicking and my blood pressure from rising. Initially, I began to reflect on the lack of support during my time of need, and then I remembered what congresswoman Waters also stated during that legendary hearing: "When you are on my time, I get to reclaim it."

I'm thankful to be in a much better place with my health, but through my health challenges I reclaimed my time by becoming more self-aware. I understand that I am likely to spend time and other precious resources on others because I have a big heart. Instead of quickly committing to helping someone with something, I now respond with, "Let me pray about it." I do just that. I pray and ask God to help me navigate what is being asked of me. Then, I wait to hear His answer. This has truly freed me from always overcommitting myself.

Depressed

I took my healing one step further by asking myself why I was putting myself last so often. This self-healing journey has revealed things about me that I did not know, nor understand. When I was sixteen years old, I became a mother. It was a troubling time for me. I carried shame and sorrow, and they were heavy. I wanted to be married. I wanted to be financially independent before bringing a child into this world. Above all, I wanted to be an adult. I was none of those things, and that caused me to be depressed.

My family was devastated by the news of my pregnancy, and my own father did not want anything to do with me. I never felt more alone in my life. With African roots, in our culture, I brought shame upon myself and my family by becoming a teenage, unwed mother. My support system stopped supporting me. I wallowed in my depression. Then, there was a shift in the way I perceived my situation. My mindset shifted from a weak one to a strong one. God blessed me with the mental strength to be not dismayed. Isaiah 41:10–11 (NIV) says, "10 So do not fear, for I am with you; do not be dismayed, for I am your God. I will strengthen you and help you; I will uphold you with my righteous right hand. 11 All who rage against you will surely be ashamed and disgraced;

those who oppose you will be as nothing and perish."

I did not know that scripture at the time, but I was living that scripture out in my real life. I decided that I would only live for God and to do my absolute best as a mother. I asked God to forgive me for my sins, and I believe that He did. I made a decision for

myself and my child to live a better life at eighteen years of age. At eighteen, I was now a legal adult. I transitioned from single parenting to SMART parenting.

I began my single parent journey alone, with two bags and a two-year-old. I walked by faith and aligned myself with other strong women. I gained strength from strong women and received a hand up, not a handout. The quote, "I come as one, but stand as 10,000," boosted by confidence. What a powerful thought, to know that you are one person standing with an army of 10,000! My family and my ancestors formed my army. I was beyond inspired and surprised to learn about my great-grandmother's soul-breaker stories on kindness and strength. Although she died in 1952, she spent her life instilling the love of God in her twelve children. Hearing her stories birthed a new confidence in me. Her blood ran through my veins, and I felt supercharged, knowing that she overcame a set of challenges in a racially intense climate. If she could get through, then so could I.

She was a woman warrior and a fighter amongst fighters. She was my shero. Through the stories about her life she taught me how to be my own shero and save myself. Grandma Mary, thank you. Your legacy lives on, and I will tell your stories until I can't anymore.

Deserving

It was time to invest in creating the best version of myself. I created several versions of myself: I have been embarrassed, I have been insecure, I have been scared, and I have been downright in despair. It was time for me to be the best version of myself. Here are some of my favorite quotes that I refer to from strong women on my first journey:

- "Students are first in education." — my first principal as an educator

- "I am reclaiming my time." — my wholistic wellness friend

- "When you act like negative people, you become them."

— my wise educator friend

- "Love is not about you."

- "Love is about what you do for others."

- "Love is so plain, even Steven Wonder can see it." — my phenomenal cousin

- "I am coming down from the mountaintop to tell every young person that is poor and working class, and has been told regardless of the color of your skin that you don't belong—don't listen to them. They don't even know how they got at those seats." — Michelle Obama

- "You won't break my soul" — Beyonce

- "In life, you have to identify charming and charasmatic people. Stay away from them charming village people girl." — my Nigerian-American friend

- "If I could change one thing in our society, I would make everyone just get along with one another, be a little kinder, and have a little empathy." — my former 4th grade star student

- "I've grown most not from victories, but setbacks. If winning is God's reward, then losing is how he teaches us." — Serena Williams

- "You are Oluwatomi." — my Nigerian Aunt

- "Get your soul right with God while you are here on earth." — my strong mom

- "Value your health and try yoga."- my loving daughter

My soul has been broken before. I was engulfed by darkness. I leaned into my "misfortune." All along, God was setting me up to go up! He was preparing me to elevate my life and the lives of others with my testimony. I've seen God's hand in my life. I've witnessed Him protect and provide for my child when I was but a child myself. He elevated me in front of those who were deliberately damaging my reputation.

He even protected me from myself. God did not do this solely for me. God has, and will, do it for anyone who believes and trusts in Him. Give it to God, and live in your calling with confidence. Whatever your tribulation is, it is not yours to be burdened with. It is only yours to give back to God. I've learned that the enemy uses minor things to distract us, in a major way, from what God has called us to do. Whatever is preventing you from activating God's guidance could be the work of the enemy.

Today, I challenge you to spend more time with God, and less time worrying. Understand the people who have been regretted the most are the ones God has selected for a specific purpose. Spend more time on your calling. Ask God how He wants to use you if you don't already know. Some people believe that your purpose is found in your passions. I believe that to be true. What are you passionate about? The answer could reveal your purpose. God healed me, and I honor Him by accepting and respecting the calling He has on my life.

I can't imagine the ramifications of not living in my purpose. Your purpose could be the gateway for others to live in their passion. When we don't live out our purpose, we not only block our blessings, but we also potentially block the blessings of those whose destinies are tied to ours. Honor God by living in your purpose.

What we tell ourselves matters. My internal voice was negative and cynical. The self-talk was damaging in so many ways. I second-guessed people, and more importantly, I second-guessed myself, my abilities, and my worth. I broke that habit by reinforcing myself with intentional, positive self-talk. I even changed the music that I listened to! I am not perfect, and I still sometimes default to negativity, but now, I recognize it! I catch myself by capturing negative thoughts and changing them to thoughts that serve me. We all have been through things that we thought would break us. We can decide to be hard on ourselves, or we can give ourselves grace and love. I choose the latter. I will continue to love myself by speaking positivity over my life and remaining phenomenally faithful. I will continue to share my testimony, release the weight of life's pain, and accept the new, rejuvenated me! I am choosing freedom. I found myself, and I am enough! I hope that you choose yourself, too.

Dear Tomi,

On your life journey, you will meet many people. Be sure to ask God for the spirit of discernment of who should be in your life for a reason, season, or lifetime. Then, when you are living life in alignment with His will, He will send you the right people to board your life train to protect, push, provide, or give you praise. Be thankful for all the beautiful loved ones, educators, spiritual advisors, leaders, doctors, and others that He will send. Love them for who they are on your life journey. Although you are the conductor, remember God is the engineer of your life train to guide you. Despite society's approval, always remember who you are and whose you are.

In life, you will face many adversities within yourself, at school, at work, in relationships. Other struggles will show up socially, emotionally, spiritually, or financially. I asked many strong women on my journey, what is essential in life? They all somewhat responded the same, "live your life and be the best version of yourself."." Be your own muse and do what sets your soul on fire! Because you are wonderfully made, do not be afraid to embrace your uniqueness. Take time to know all of you, even if that means forgiving and restoring broken relationships for self-discovery.

Overall, if I could reclaim time as a twenty-four-year-old woman. I would know that I am "Tomi" and follow the advice my mother has been trying to teach me my entire life. Unfortunately, I could not receive it until I fought for my life in the hospital. I realized ninety percent of the things and people I wasted time worrying about did not matter. I should have been more worried about my "SOUL." I could have received my mother's advice if I had valued myself more at twenty-four. At the age of forty, I now live by the words my Aunt Moji would say, "You are Tomi."

Toyin Fadina

Chapter 12

Little Fires Everywhere

In March 2020, Kerry Washington produced and starred in the TV series, *Little Fires Everywhere*. It was a drama-filled series about how two families' lives collide and how the implications of each person's personal situation contributed to the fires that were sparked both figuratively and literally. I binge-watched the series from start to finish in just a few days. That says a lot because I don't often watch television, but occasionally, I get hooked on a good storyline. As an author and publisher, I watch TV for the story, and a good story makes me forget all of the tasks that I need to complete. I become one with the couch as I just lie in front of the screen and immerse myself with the film. My sister, Lexie, was watching the series and asked me to join her. As I watched the show, it dawned on me that I had my own drama-filled story unfolding right before me filled with plot twists, climaxes, and a mix of co-stars that added to the story of my life.

2020 was a life-changing year for the entire world. The way it changed mine made me think that I would never be the same, and looking back over these two years since 2020, I was right. I am not the same person emotionally, mentally, and especially spiritually. In a short period of time, I was surrounded by these little fires. Incapable of putting them out myself, I realized that my life needed a lot more faith in God.

A state, process, or instance of combustion in which fuel or other material is ignited and combined with oxygen, giving off light, heat, and flame… that's how the Oxford dictionary defines fire. Here's how little fires in my life nearly burned down my sanity.

When the pandemic hit, I was working as a full-time entrepreneur. With the world shutting down, people were left with very few options: You either worked from home, inherited the title of an essential worker, or became unemployed because hundreds of thousands of companies were laying people off.

The Coronavirus, or COVID-19, seemed to come out of nowhere, and it swept through the lungs of millions and killed nearly 400,000 people across the world. Everything was so uncertain. Groceries and household needs were scarce, curfews were set, the stock market crashed, and children could only attend school virtually.

I remember thinking, *How am I going to survive as a publisher and author?* People were saving what money they had because of the financial crisis the world was in. Who would want to write and publish a book at a time like this? I was not saving like I should have prior to the pandemic, so I did not have a cushion to fall back on during it.

I began to stress about money more. I didn't want to check my account balance, I already knew that the amount was not enough, no matter what the numerical value was. I cut back on spending, and started heavily considering shutting down BFF Publishing House just so that I could find a full-time job that would give me the financial security that I needed to take care of my daughter Jett and myself. Just as fast as the thought entered my mind is as quickly as it left. People began to call and schedule consultations via our website. A common response that I received was, "Now that I have the time because of the pandemic, I can finally write and publish my book." Although I didn't look at the pandemic that way, so many people did, and it made sense—we all had a lot more time at home. People were finally able to do what they had been putting off due to the lack of time during their busy pre-pandemic lives.

My mom has what feels like a million sayings that she uses and over the years; I hear myself repeating what I have heard over my lifetime. "Ye of little faith," I said to myself as I looked at the increase in book publishing. The saying means that you don't have faith in something or you don't believe in a person.

I was overjoyed with the business and felt terrible that I did not trust God would not come through when the truth of the matter is, He has not failed me. I am grateful that God's mercy showed up even when I doubted that it would. If it were not so, you would not be reading this book that you are holding in your hand.

I've learned that when things get tough and you can't see a way out, it's all just a matter of your faith and how much of the circumstance or problem that begs the question: Are you willing to truly give it to God? Once you give it all to God, you open up your head, heart, and hands to receive not only the sense of true freedom, but all that He has to offer—which I can assure you is better than your best-case scenario.

The Expert Extinguisher:

Do you know how to extinguish a fire? To effectively extinguish a fire, one of three elements of the fire must be removed. Those elements are oxygen, heat, and fuel. If an object is combustible, it is fuel for a fire—paper, wood, gas, etc. Cooling the fire by drenching it with water is the most popular method. There are also other extinguishing methods, such as starving and smothering fires.

In the expert extinguisher section of my chapter, I am going to explain how God put out the little fires in my life according to His word and how He can do the same in your life.

Deuteronomy 28:11–12:

"And the Lord shall make thee plenteous in goods, in the fruit of thy body, and in the fruit of thy cattle, and in the fruit of thy ground, in the land which the Lord swore unto thy fathers to give thee."

"The Lord shall open unto thee his good treasure, the heaven to give the rain unto thy land in his season, and to bless all the work of thine hand: and thou shalt lend unto many nations, and thou shalt not borrow."

Philippians 4:19:

"And my God will supply every need of yours according to His riches in glory in Christ Jesus."

Psalms 84:11:

"For the Lord God is a sun and shield;

The Lord will give grace and glory;

No good thing will He withhold

From those who walk uprightly."

Use This Prayer When Facing Financial Blockage:

Heavenly Father,

I come to You as humbly as I know how, Lord. Father, You know my financial situation, and I invite You to increase my wealth. Lord, You are Jehova Jira. You have always provided for me, and I trust Your unchanging hands. I ask that You multiply every dollar that I have, pressed down, shaking together, and running over as Your word promises. Lord, it is my heart's desire to be the giver and not the borrower. As Your child, I know that I am a Kingdom child, and I stretch out my hands out for You to fill them until they overflow. Lord God, remove any ill intentions from my heart and please forgive me for any times that I have shown myself less than worthy of Your blessings. Bless me now, Lord. I claim financial freedom, and I bind financial hardship never to rise up against me again. All of my bills are paid on time. My credit score is 800. I make intelligent investments. My money works for me! Thank You, Lord, for turning my situation around.

In Jesus's name,

Amen.

"Dad, what does it feel like to call someone else your name?" I asked my father.

"It feels amazing," he smiled.

I was named after my father, Anthony Mutcherson. He was affectionately called Tony Boy or Tony. Not only did we share the same name, we shared several interests like art, making people laugh, spending time with our family, and enjoying good food—especially crab boils! We also look just alike! As a child, people called me his twin, and as an adult, some of my family members that thought that they were funny would call me Tony Boy jokingly. Even I saw it and recognized our strong resemblance. When people tell me that I look like someone, I am usually very doubtful because I don't see the resemblance, but with my dad, there was just no denying it. You can only imagine how I felt when one of my very best friends and father called me to tell me that he had a life-threatening condition.

The beginning of the end started in April of 2020. I'll always remember that day. I was stuck in Atlanta traffic, driving to pick Jett and Logan up from school. My cell phone rang and I answered my dad's call.

"Hey, Daughter," he said.

"Hey, Dad. How you doing?" I responded.

"Not so great," he said in a melancholy tone.

He had me call all of my siblings on three-way so that he could tell us his news all at the same time.

"I have stage four cancer," he said.

His words echoed in my ear. I heard him, but I didn't. My eyes darted all around. My eyes welled, and my throat was burning. I was in yet another fire.

I was completely dismayed. There was no warning, no slow progression. What happened to the three stages that came before the fourth one? It was all so sudden, the most unpleasant surprise. I tried to compose myself and tried to find the right words to say in response. What do people say in times like this, especially when it's to someone who has had the right words to say in my times of need? I swallowed my tears.

"We're going to beat it," I said shakingly. I said it again, more confidently. I wanted to be hopeful and I wanted to be strong. I had faith that he could, and that he would, beat his cancer.

Just when I got my Dad back, there was a strong possibility that I was going to lose him, this time forever. My mom often shared the story of how I was at their wedding. She was pregnant with me at the time. Their wedding pictures were timeless. My mother was breathtakingly beautiful, and my dad was dapper. Those pretty pictures were just that, pretty pictures. My memories of them together are scarce. I was a young girl when my parents first separated and then divorced soon after.

He was addicted to drugs. That addiction transformed him into someone that was unrecognizable. He loved us so much, but when the drugs came into play, he didn't love anyone or anything like he did chasing a high. It's the typical 1980s story. Drugs tore our family apart and derailed not only my dad's life, but the lives of millions of others during that decade. He was no longer a responsible adult, and his poor choices led him into the prison system. For half of my life, my dad was in and out of prison. He missed important life events.

Then, in 2017, my Dad was released from prison and moved in with me and Lexie. At the time, we were living in a beautiful townhouse in Tallahassee, pursuing our MBAs from Florida A&M University. This was one of the most special times in my life. We finally had our father with us. We made so many precious memories. He taught Jett and Logan about all types of things. We talked, cooked together, went places together, and we all just loved on each other. I learned a lot about my dad. I got to see him as an evolved and God-fearing man.

What I loved most about my dad was his big heart. He went out of his way to put a smile on your face. He didn't have much, but whatever he had, he would just give it away, even to strangers. He was one of my biggest supporters, tying first place with my mom. I remember when he was in prison and how he asked me to send him some of the books that I wrote so that he could sell them for me... in prison! He really sold my children's books to prisoners and sent me the money. Then, when we lived together, he would sell my books out of his car and give me the money. He was really proud of me, and it showed.

Cancer caused my dad so much physical pain. My dad's cancer caused me emotional and mental pain. On October 2, 2021, my Father took his last breath. I was at a cheerleading event for Jett when I got the call from the doctor. Although I expected that I would receive that dreadful call, I was not ready to lose my father. Thankfully, my mom and sister were in town. They were all at the game, and even my boyfriend, and La'Dreauna, affectionately known as Dre was there, too. We prayed together and spoke of the good times. It was a difficult day, but it wasn't as dark as I knew it could have been because we were there for one another.

My father not being here with me is an incalculable loss. I am still grieving for my father. I still have his phone number saved on my favorites list. I still cry for him. I still talk to him like he is here with me, because he *is* here with me. I feel his presence, and I pray that I always do. Toni Morrison once said, "Something that is loved is never lost." I love you, Dad. Thank you.

The Expert Extinguisher:

Psalm 34:18:

"The Lord is close to the brokenhearted and saves those who are crushed in spirit."

John 14:1–4:

"[1] Let not your heart be troubled; you believe in God, believe also in Me. [2] In My Father's house are many mansions; if it were not so, I would have told you. I go to prepare a place for you. [3] And if I go and prepare a place for you, I will come again and receive you to Myself; that where I am, there you may be also. ⁴ And where I go you know, and the way you know."

Use This Prayer When Facing the Death of a Loved One:

Heavenly Father,

Thank you for the life of {insert name}. Thank you for all of the blessings that You sent through him/her. {insert name} was my best friend, and Lord, I feel lost without him/her here with me. My heart is filled with a pain that I have never felt before. I need You to carry me through these restless nights and lonely days. I don't understand why You allowed this to happen, but I trust You. I miss him/her beyond measure, but I trust You.

Lord God, grant me the serenity that only You can provide. Lord, grant me peace. Lord, grant me strength. Have mercy on me and my family. Show me how to grieve. Send Your angels as I navigate not having {insert name} here in the flesh. Comfort me, Lord, by flooding me with images of him/her next to You in perfect health.

These things I ask in Your Son Jesus's name,

Amen.

Little Fire III

I found out that I was pregnant in October of 2020. I was completely surprised and utterly thrilled. I had been wanting another child for a long time, but I was just not sure if it would happen for me again. After several failed relationships and being unwed, I was trying to accept that I may have one child. Although I never wanted my daughter to be an only child, time was getting away from me. She was eight years old at the time, and she wanted me to have a baby more than I did! She would constantly ask me to have a baby, on a daily basis. It would sadden me tremendously when I told her that was not up to me; I wanted a husband to make a baby.

Now that I was pregnant, I was elated and a little nervous. I had not had a baby in eight years, which seemed like a very long time for me. In the time it took me to decide that I was more joyful than nervous, I began to bleed. I remember going to the bathroom to urinate and seeing one tiny drop of blood in the toilet as I turned to flush. It made that nervous feeling resurface. I stared at it for what seemed like forever because I knew the possibility of its presence.

The next morning, I made an appointment with a random gynecologist to gain some insight on what was going on inside of my body. Several places were booked for same day and next day appointments so I was relieved to finally find an available one.

I began to get ready for my appointment and I saw a little more blood, this time on the tissue that I wiped with. I cried and continued to prepare myself for my appointment. The first place that I went to was someplace out of a 1990s movie screen. That may have been the last time it had been remodeled, if at all. The building had lost its natural tan color and it was now dull, with splatters of green spots accompanied by moss growing all around it. The once electric door now non-operational propped open to allow clients easy access into and out of the building. I sighed and entered the building. Greeted by the heat before I could reach the receptionist, I noticed the other women in the waiting room fanning themselves with paper, magazines, or just their hands. They were all miserably enduring the wait to be seen.

"Hello! I'll be right with you," the receptionist's voice interrupted my careful observation of the room.

"Yes, ma'am," I managed to muster up now that I had reached her desk.

"Do you have an appointment?" she turned back around from the filing cabinet and asked.

"Yes. I am Antionette Mutcherson."

"I see you here," she responded, not looking up from her computer screen. "What brings you in today?"

"I recently found out that I am pregnant, and yesterday, I saw a small amount of blood in the toilet yesterday. Today, there was a little more."

That response got her attention, I guess, because for the first time, she looked up at me and our eyes connected.

"I'm sorry to hear that. Have a seat over there and fill out this new patient paperwork. The nurse will be with you soon."

"Okay, I said, feeling my throat tighten and my eyes welling up."

Not now, Toni. This is not where you want to fall apart, I told myself. I took a deep breath and sat down on the front row so as to not have to watch the pregnant women and their bellies remind me why I was here in the first place.

Thankfully, in a matter of minutes, a young lady in her mid- to late-twenties with cornrows opened the door and called my name with a concerned smile on her face.

"Yes," I answered, walking towards her.

She walked me to the front door on the right. "You can have a seat here," she said, pointing to the black chair against the wall. Then, she sat down across from me.

"I'm so sorry, but we do not have the ultrasound machine to examine you. The doctor can see you and ask questions, but I wanted to tell you that so you could decide to be seen or not."

I was becoming more and more hopeless. I decided not to be seen by the doctor, so I left.

When I got home, I turned my feelings off the best that I could so that my daughter and my niece would not be alarmed. My sister, Lexie, had relocated to Phoenix, Arizona to start a business, and I was keeping my niece, Logan, as she got things situated. I never told them that I was pregnant. I did not want to get their hopes up, nor did I want to explain why there was no baby inside of me anymore. The two of them together were like walking Black girl magic. Although they are first cousins, they declared that they are sisters long ago, and that's how they introduce themselves to others. They had such a strong resemblance that people often asked if they were sisters. Their love, laughter, and support for each other could almost convince me too! They were such sweet, pure, joyous girls. I could not crush their little hearts with my heartbreaking news. I got myself together, did homework with them, and made dinner. It was a very difficult time in my life to manage my feelings, and my responsibilities.

At this time, I had only told a handful of people about the pregnancy: my boyfriend, Lexie; my mom; my sister, Vandora; and Dre. I told each of them at different parts of my journey, and they all offered love and support. I am forever grateful for that.

Each time that I went to the restroom, there was more blood. Instead of waiting until the next appointment, I decided to go to the emergency room. Going to the emergency room was not an easy decision to make. We were in the midst of the pandemic, and people were dying in astronomical numbers from COVID-19. The hospitals were flooded with COVID-19 patients, and most were severely understaffed. I was really scared to go to the emergency room because of the potential COVID exposure.

There I was, walking into Piedmont Hospital with my boyfriend by my side. I don't know if it was the mask that I was wearing at the time that was restricting my breathing or if it was my nerves, but every breath I took felt heavy. I had to exert extreme effort. This involuntary action now required me to act. It was as if I was taking deep, intentional breaths, but I was not, and yet, that was the outcome. I was settling into my circumstance. Scared. *What would I do once the doctors told me that in which I was fearing? How would I walk out of there? How would I exist without the one I never got to know?* These thoughts poured into my mind, and then onto my cheeks. I cried all of the time, even now as I write this chapter for you.

Sitting in the physical waiting room, I thought about how

much of my life I spent sitting in a metaphorical waiting room. I waited on financial freedom, love, and success, and there I was, waiting to learn if the baby that I had also been waiting for would live. The sound of my name brought me back to my reality. The nurse escorted me to the exam room and directed me to the restroom inside the room.

"Take everything off and put on the gown. Don't pee if you can help it. A full bladder helps with the ultrasound."

She handed me the hospital gown, and I disrobed and did as I was instructed.

The room was dim and cold. I laid down on the exam table and watched her set up her machine. She asked me several questions and input my responses into her chart. She squeezed a cool, clear gel on my womb and placed her tool on my belly.

"I am going to take several pictures, and then the doctor will analyze them and go over the results with you."

I understood what she said—or maybe I did not, because I still asked, "is something wrong?"

She repeated herself, "The doctor will go over these images with you once I am done."

The process was long, and I was anxious. It was miserable. What felt like hours passed, and all at once, she was satisfied with her progress. She wiped the gel off my stomach and released me back to the restroom, where I put my clothes back on and urinated. I wiped, saw blood, and teared up—a new ritual that could not be escaped.

I went back to the waiting room. Waited. Then, real hours, not by any stretch of my imagination, passed, and I was finally called back to a makeshift hallway room. This small space was enclosed by a white curtain room divider. I guess this was because the hospitals were overflowing with COVID patients and there were no more rooms available, so, as a result, they began to create space where they could.

To my surprise, they told me that everything appeared

to be okay: "Sometimes, women bleed at the beginning of their pregnancy." They told me that I should not be alarmed. I thought that I was dreaming. The doctor had captured my human chorionic gonadotropin (hCG) level and referred me to an OB/GYN at Piedmont to visit in a few days to see if my hCG was increasing or decreasing. If it was increasing, that meant the baby was growing. If it was decreasing, that meant I was having a miscarriage.

It was a miracle! I was going to be okay; my baby was going to be okay. I exhaled at the realization that everything was fine. My body could and would be a safe home for my baby to safely develop and receive nourishment in. In this single moment, my faith was restored, and I could breathe again, involuntarily.

When the day came for me to visit the referred OB/GYN and my hCG levels were compared, it was finally revealed to me that I was indeed losing my baby. There was no reversing this process. I just had to allow my body to continue the process of passing the embryo by bleeding out. It was one of the darkest days of my life. The doctor's words rang into my ears for days.

It was late in the morning when I returned home. I sunk into myself and dreaded interacting with anyone. I walked into my house and sat still as a stone on my couch as I tried to make sense of it all. *What did I do wrong? Why is this happening to me? Am I dreaming? Will I be able to have more kids?* I had more questions than answers, and that grieved me even more. All I wanted to do was to sit and make myself at home with my depression. I could not. I did not have the luxury of not working.

I had clients that needed to speak with me or needed responses to their emails, or needed their book published. My life was still vibrantly active, even though a part of me was actively dying. I did my best to balance it all out.

Thank God, I had told Dre. I often tell her that she is more like my mom than any of my mom's actual children. They are both sweet and purehearted. I can only give God the glory for their disposition because it is nothing short of miraculous that they have not been jaded by the world like most other people. I did not want to tell her because I did not want her to worry, a trait that she and my mother share. But there was no hiding it from Dre. She and I were roommates. One Friday night, I sat alone in the dark on the living room couch, focusing on the darkness within me, and she came home unexpectedly. She illuminated the room when she walked in. By the time she entered, I could not quickly alter my disposition, nor could I reach the light switch.

"Girl, you scared me. Why are you sitting in the dark?" she questioned, but before I could answer, she continued to walk closer, and my despair was realized. She hugged me and I melted into her arms.

"I am having a miscarriage," I sobbed out my declaration.

Shocked and saddened by my news, she began to cry, too. From that moment on, she took on my duties as a mother and aunt. She got the girls ready for virtual school, helped with homework, cooked, and cleaned—all of this so that I could keep to myself and mourn, or work from my bed, or cry in peace. This selfless act saved me in more ways than one, and I am forever grateful to her for that. Thank you, Dre.

On Tuesday, November 3, 2020, I had the saddest birthday yet. This was the first of its kind. My birthday is a special day for obvious reasons; everyone loves being celebrated and being blessed enough to see another year, but my birthday is also special because I was born on my paternal grandmother's birthday. I typically take a trip, host a dinner, or do something with my family and close friends. I was still in the middle of miscarrying. The only gift that I wanted, I could not have. In my family, birthdays are a big deal, especially for the kids in the family. Jett and Logan were so excited about my approaching birthday; it was all they talked about leading up to my birthday. I could not disappoint them with my disposition, so I pulled myself together and decided to be grateful for another year of life, despite my circumstances.

My mother and I had recently talked about how children are a blessing, especially when you are sad. She said, "When you have children in your life, it gives you the opportunity to think of others, and it almost forces you to focus on something beyond your circumstance. Children have their childlike optimism that can elevate your vibration if you allow yourself to be present with them." I found this to be true on my birthday that year.

Jett and Logan instructed my boyfriend on all the things to get me for my birthday, and he went out and purchased the items the night before. The next morning on my birthday, they insisted that I stay upstairs until they came and got me. When they did come to beckon me from my room, they could barely contain themselves.

"Close your eyes, Mommy," Jett said, placing her hand in mine to guide me downstairs into the kitchen area. When she told me that I could open them, life was pumped back into my body. I was resuscitated by their joy. I opened my eyes to find balloons, a dozen red roses, and all of my favorite breakfast items organized beautifully on the dining room table. They had breakfast potatoes, veggie sausage, fresh fruit, and sparkling cider. Dre, Jett, Logan, and my boyfriend were all wearing big smiles in addition to their birthday hats. It was not only perfect, but just what I needed.

I decided to be present in that moment. I vibrated higher with every smile, laugh, and loving gesture. There is a lot of power in being present. The present moment truly does feel like a gift if you decide to only concern yourself with the things that are happening right in front of you. Being present requires that you leave the past in the past and that you take no thought for the future. So often, I have fallen victim to being physically somewhere, but my thoughts have time traveled back to a painful memory or a dreadful future worry.

There is so much freedom in being present. I encourage you to take advantage of the present moment, because when you do not, it robs you of the joy in that moment. I have done that so many times, and I usually regret that I did not savor the seconds that I can never get back. We have over 6,000 thoughts in a day. That is a lot of real estate for the Lord to give you inspirational, peaceful, and positive thoughts if you stay present to receive them.

I fed on their love like it was spinach and I was Popeye.

It carried me through the next few days as the miscarriage completed its process. Eventually, that nourishment to my soul tapered off as the days grew longer. The bleeding had subsided, but the event itself found a permanent place in my heart and mind until piece by painful piece I gave it all to God.

The Expert Extinguisher:

Joshua 1:9:

"Have I not commanded you? Be strong and courageous. Do not be frightened, and do not be dismayed, for the Lord your God is with you wherever you go."

Philippians 4:6–8:

"Do not be anxious about anything, but in everything by prayer and supplication with thanksgiving, let your requests be made known to God. And the peace of God, which surpasses all understanding, will guard your hearts and your minds in Christ Jesus. Finally, brothers, whatever is true, whatever is honorable, whatever is just, whatever is pure, whatever is lovely, whatever is commendable, if there is any excellence, if there is anything worthy of praise, think about these things."

Use This Prayer When Facing Loss:

Lord God,

I need You right now. I need You to hold my hand and heal my heart as I find my way. I am lost in what feels like a sea of pain. I don't know what to do with all of this pain that is inside of me. I don't know how not to think about what I could have done differently. While I don't know these things, I trust that You do. Teach me, Heavenly Father. Teach me how to accept the things that I do not understand and that I cannot change. Release me of the feeling of depression and defeat. Show me how to embrace the change that You have allowed to happen. Thank You for the time shared with {insert name}. Thank You for joy-filled memories that I can revisit and smile. And lastly, thank You for the friends and family that I have with me. Help me to nourish those relationships. Keep them safe.

This I ask in Jesus's name,

Amen.

Little Fire IV

One cold day in December, I was on the phone with my sister, Lexie. We are extremely close, so we talk every day, especially since she was living in Phoenix. I don't remember much about what my sister said on that call before she announced, "I'm pregnant," or even what she said afterwards while we were on a Facetime call. I began to look like what I was going through. I did not do my hair, I did not put make-up on, I did not wear pretty clothes. I remember being really excited for her! We had both talked about having more children. I was genuinely happy for my little sister. She loves children, and she is so good with babies, even better than I am! I have always felt that way.

When we got off the phone, I felt the anger and despair building up inside of me.

"God, why did You allow the timeline of our lives to unfold the way it did? Why couldn't I have a healthy baby? Was there something wrong with me? What caused the miscarriage?"

The more questions I asked, the more frustrated I felt.

I would have loved for Lexie and I to have been pregnant together. That had always been a dream of ours. We witnessed it firsthand with our aunts, Nicole and Treemonisha. We were young girls then, but it was so beautiful to see. That was not going to be our story. I had just lost my baby a month before my sister found out that she was pregnant.

Initially, I thought the worst of the situation. I thought that I would have to watch her belly grow the way mine did not. I thought that I would have to watch my niece or nephew celebrate a birthday every year and be reminded that my unborn child would be the same age. My little light that usually shines and brings joy to others when I enter a room was nonexistent. I was clinically depressed.

My boyfriend told me that it was time to get professional help. He was right; I needed therapy. I had completely lost myself in a sea of grief. I could no longer help myself. I was too upset with God to lean on His help, and I was too embarrassed to talk to friends and family members about losing my child. Looking for an available therapist in the middle of a pandemic was like looking for a needle in a haystack.

Everyone was going through something, whether it was losing family members, losing jobs, or losing their minds from staying home all of the time. It was a tough time for the entire human race. That reflected in the surge of new business in the mental healthcare industry. It took me months to find my therapist. Unfortunately, I had never had therapy before, and I did not know a lot about it. I wanted a Black Christian woman who had experience with dealing with grief AND who was based in Atlanta, Georgia.

Shar'ron was, and still is, a godsend. She checked all of my boxes. When I finally found her, I still had to wait to be put on her calendar. I was counting down the days until I spoke with her. It gave me something to look forward to. I was going to have my own person who I could talk to about the miscarriage, the sadness, and the anger without overkilling the topic. I definitely talked to my circle about it to no end, or I concealed my true feelings by pretending that I was okay so that they would not have to worry about how much of a wreck I truly was.

My circumstance had completely consumed me. Everywhere that I went, I saw a baby or a pregnant woman. Every movie that I watched had a baby or a pregnant woman in it; on social media, I experienced the same thing. I felt like I could not escape babies. They were on my radar, and I picked them up with every step that I made.

Our first session was via the phone. I cried and cried as I tried to fill her in on the details of my dreadful situation. She was patient with me and guided me along a path that allowed me to be patient with myself. My biggest issue was that I did not know where to put the pain. I carried it all the time everywhere that I went. She also encouraged me to write a letter to my unborn child. That was the pivotal point for me. That empowered me to put the pain somewhere. I was now releasing myself of the suffering. It was the perfect suggestion for me as a writer. Growing up, I gravitated to writing when I needed to express myself to my friends and family. I wrote so many letters to my mother apologizing for one thing or another. Today, I still enjoy writing letters.

The letter to my unborn child was one of the most important letters that I had ever written. I poured my heart into the letter below:

Dear My Little Angel,

I am so sorry that we didn't have a chance to meet. It's been a real painful regret that I have. I am your mother. I am Antionette Mutcherson, but everyone calls me Toni. I would have loved to see your beautiful face and love on you every day of your life. Although we never got a chance to meet, I still love you. I am so sorry for not being able to keep you with me. I am so sorry that Jett did not get to meet you. You both would have been in love with each other. Jett would have been your big sister. She has the biggest heart I have ever seen in such a little person.

I often imagine what you look like, your smile, what sex you were, and what your personality would have been like. I pray that you can forgive me… I pray that I can forgive myself. I have changed a lot from losing you. There's this void in my heart and in my life. There is so much I wish that I could say to you, but it's hard for me to find the words.

I have blamed myself ever since the first drop of blood that I saw. It seems so unfair, and it's unbelievable at times. It is so hard to say goodbye to you, but I must. I will hold you in my heart always, and I look forward to meeting you someday in Heaven. We will be reunited once more, my love.

Until we meet again.

Love,

Mom

I felt compelled to apologize for not being able to keep him or her safe, and for not being able to meet. It was the sweetest goodbye that I could think of. I finally felt some relief. I set us both free in my heart.

The feeling of freedom and forgiveness snowballed. Each day, I felt a little better and a little stronger. I'm not completely healed, to be honest, and that's okay. I have made my peace with my miscarriage. What gives me peace is God's promise to give us the desires of our hearts. He knows that I want more kids. Without a doubt, He is going to fulfill that for me. That is my phenomenal faith. I'll never be the same because of my miscarriage, but I will always lean on God as the perils of life present themselves.

The Expert Extinguisher:

Revelation 21:4:

"He will wipe away every tear from their eyes, and death shall be no more, neither shall there be mourning, nor crying, nor pain anymore, for the former things have passed away."

Philippians 4:6–7:

"Do not be anxious about anything, but in every situation, by prayer and petition, with thanksgiving, present your requests to God. And the peace of God, which transcends all understanding, will guard your hearts and your minds in Christ Jesus."

John 14:27:

"Peace I leave with you; my peace I give to you. Not as the world gives do I give to you. Let not your hearts be troubled, neither let them be afraid."

Use This Prayer When Facing Comparison and Depression:

Dear Lord,

Thank You for showing me what You are capable of doing in my life by granting me the opportunity to witness what You are doing in the lives of others. Lord, forgive me for comparing their circumstance to mine. Lord, hold me in Your arms and soothe my aching heart. I am in a dark place that only You can shed light on. Shine Your light on me right now. Shine so brightly that I only see You. I claim the victory right now that Your plan for my life is better than any want or desire I can dream up. Thank You for blessing {insert the person that you are thinking of}! Thank You for showing me that if You are blessing my friends and family, then You are in my neighborhood! I am next in line for Your grace and favor. VICTORY TODAY IS MINE!

This, and all things, I ask in your Son Jesus's name,

Amen.

There will be fires—big and small fires—that blaze unexpectedly, unknowingly, and uninvited. I pray that you lean not on your own understanding. Instead, lean on the Expert Extinguisher. He can put out any fire that rises against you. He saw it coming, and He can protect you from it. God loves you. Don't just keep the faith; nurture it so that it can be a phenomenal resource in your times of adversity.

Antionette "Toni" Mutcherson

Made in the USA
Columbia, SC
27 November 2022